YORK NO

D0120674

TOUCHING THE VOID

JOE SIMPSON

NOTES BY RACHEAL SMITH

Longman
is an imprint of

PEARSON

York Press

The right of Racheal Smith to be identified as Author of this Work has been asserted by her in accordance with the Copyright, Designs and Patents Act 1988

YORK PRESS
322 Old Brompton Road, London SW5 9JH

PEARSON EDUCATION LIMITED
Edinburgh Gate, Harlow,
Essex CM20 2JE, United Kingdom
Associated companies, branches and representatives throughout the world

First published 2010

10 9 8 7 6 5 4 3 2 1

ISBN 978–1–4082–4884–3

Illustrations by Mike Lacey; and Neil Gower (p. 6 only)
Photograph of Joe Simpson by kind permission of Photos 12/Alamy

Phototypeset by Border Consultants, Dorset

Printed in the UK

CONTENTS

PART FOUR
KEY CONTEXTS AND THEMES

PART FIVE
LANGUAGE AND STRUCTURE

PART SIX
GRADE BOOSTER

PART ONE: INTRODUCTION

Study and revision advice

There are two main stages to your reading and work on *Touching the Void*. Firstly, the study of the book as you read it. Secondly, your preparation or revision for exam or controlled assessment. These top tips will help you with both.

READING AND STUDYING THE BOOK – DEVELOP INDEPENDENCE!

- Try to engage and respond **personally** to the characters, ideas and story – not just for your enjoyment, but also because it helps you develop your own **independent ideas** and **thoughts** about *Touching the Void*. This is something that examiners are very keen to see.

- **Talk** about the text with friends and family; ask questions in class; put forward your own viewpoint – and, if you have time, **read around** the text to find out about *Touching the Void*.

- Take time to **consider** and **reflect** on the **key elements** of the book; keep your own notes, mind-maps, diagrams, scribbled jottings about the characters and how you respond to them; follow the story as it progresses (what do you think might happen?); discuss the main themes and ideas (what do *you* think it is about? Adventure? Friendship? Loneliness?); pick out language that impresses you or makes an **impact**, and so on.

- Treat your studying **creatively**. When you write essays or give talks about the book make your responses creative. Think about using really clear ways of explaining yourself, use unusual **quotations**, well-chosen **vocabulary**, and try powerful, persuasive ways of beginning or ending what you say or write.

REVISION – DEVELOP ROUTINES AND PLANS!

- **Good revision** comes from **good planning**. Find out when your exam or controlled assessment is and then plan to look at key aspects of *Touching the Void* on different days or times during your revision period. You could use these Notes – see **How can these Notes help me?** – and add dates or times when you are going to cover a particular topic.

- Use **different ways** of **revising**. Sometimes talking about the text and what you know/don't know with a friend or member of the family can help; other times, filling a sheet of A4 with all your ideas in different colour pens about a character, for example Joe, can make ideas come alive; other times, making short lists of quotations to learn, or numbering events in the plot can assist you.

- **Practise plans** and **essays**. As you get nearer the 'day', start by looking at essay **questions** and writing short bulleted plans. Do several plans (you don't have to write the whole essay); then take those plans and add details to them (quotations, linked ideas). Finally, using the advice in **Part Six: Grade Booster**, write some practice essays and then check them out against the advice we have provided.

> **EXAMINER'S TIP**
>
> Prepare for the exam/ assessment! Whatever you need to bring, make sure you have it with you – books, if you're allowed, pens, pencils – and that you turn up on time!

Introducing *Touching the Void*

SETTING

Siula Grande is a mountain in the Cordillera Huayhuash, in the Peruvian Andes. It was first climbed in 1936 via the north face. The west face was not successfully climbed before Simpson and Yates made their ascent in 1985.

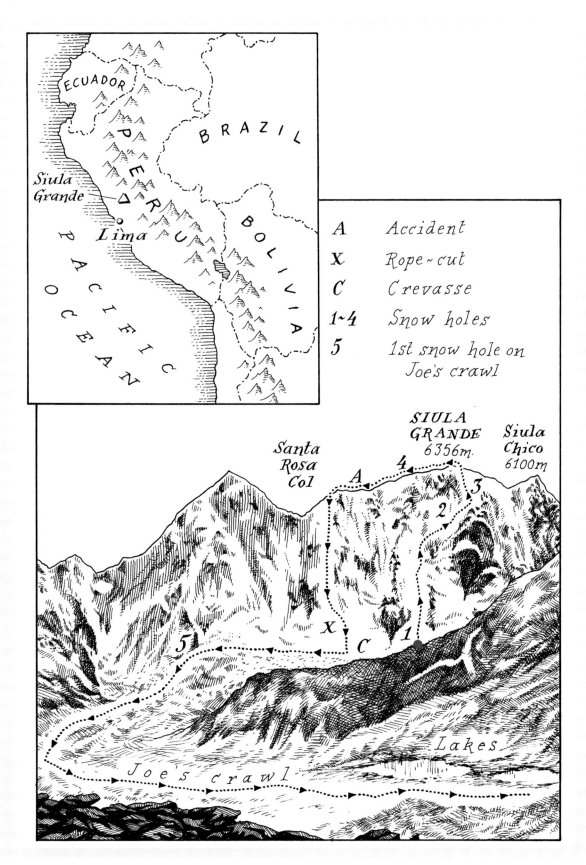

A   Accident
X   Rope-cut
C   Crevasse
1-4   Snow holes
5   1st snow hole on Joe's crawl

CHARACTERS: WHO'S WHO

Joe Simpson   Simon Yates   Richard Hawkings

JOE SIMPSON: AUTHOR AND CONTEXT

1936 Siula Grande in the Peruvian Andes first climbed by Germans Arnold Awerzger and Erwin Schneider via the north face

1960 Joe Simpson born in Kuala Lumpa, where his father was stationed in the army

1985 Becomes the first climber, along with Simon Yates, to ascend the west face of Siula Grande; there was controversy at the time of the accident, as Yates cut the rope that bound him to Simpson – something that many climbers believe breaks the code of climbers

1988 *Touching the Void* published

2003 Film of the book released; Simpson claims he chose to recount the events because he wanted to defend the actions of his friend

– present Simpson's survival has become part of mountaineering folklore; he still lives in Sheffield, and is a mountaineer, author and motivational speaker

PART TWO: Plot and Action

Plot summary: What happens in *Touching the Void*?

REVISION ACTIVITY

- Go through the summary lists below and **highlight** what you think is the **key moment** in each section.
- Then find each moment in the **text** and **reread** it. Write down **two reasons** why you think each moment is so **important**.

CHAPTER 1

- All the characters are at base camp in the Peruvian Andes getting used to the conditions.
- We are introduced to Simon and Richard.
- Simon and Joe make several test climbs but each time fail to reach their objective.
- Richard, Simon and Joe walk to the beginning of the climb.
- Richard is left behind when the going becomes dangerous.
- Simon and Joe begin the ascent.

CHAPTERS 2–3

- Joe and Simon enjoy the climb at first.
- Later, Joe and Simon climb in the dark with no ice screw.
- They manage to make it into a snow hole and sleep.
- They are optimistic about the rest of the climb when they see it gets easier.
- They reach the summit.
- They begin the descent and a bad storm begins.
- Simon falls off the ridge but is saved by the rope.

CHAPTERS 4–5

- They walk over an overhanging cornice.
- Joe sees a crack in the ice and feels afraid.
- Joe falls down the ice cliff and drives his thigh bone through his knee joint.
- Simon reaches Joe and believes that Joe will not survive.
- While Simon climbs back up to free the ropes, Joe makes an attempt to get moving.
- They keep going rather than make a snow hole for the night.
- They set up a rope system to lower Joe down the slope.

CHAPTERS 6–8

- The slope becomes steeper.
- Joe realises too late that the slope is reaching a cliff.
- Joe falls over the edge and is unable to get back up.
- Simon feels Joe fall, waits and then realises he must carry on lowering him because he has no hope of pulling him back up.
- Simon can lower Joe no more and decides to cut the rope because they would both die if he didn't.
- Joe falls into a crevasse and lands on a snow bridge.
- Believing Joe is dead, Simon then continues to descend alone and meets Richard.

CHAPTERS 9–11

- After many hours Joe abseils down into the crevasse, realising he cannot stay on the bridge and live.
- He hits the floor and manages to climb out even though he has a badly broken leg and has just fallen nearly 100 feet from the ice bridge.
- He then slides uncontrollably down the glacier.
- Joe hears a voice that forces him to keep going and to dig snow holes when he needs to sleep.
- At base camp, Simon sorts through Joe's belongings and burns his clothes.
- While hopping through the boulders, desperately in need of water, Joe recalls events and songs from his past.

CHAPTERS 12–13

- After a few days while Simon recovers, Richard begins to insist that he and Simon should leave.
- Meanwhile, Joe is in the river basin and losing energy.
- Simon agrees to Richard's suggestion that he organise locals to help them leave the next morning.
- Night arrives and Joe continues stumbling in the dark shouting Simon's name.
- In the morning, Simon hears Joe and helps him back to base camp.
- Simon and Richard organise mules to take Joe down the mountain the next day.
- The book ends with Joe in hospital where he has an operation.

Chapter 1: Beneath the Mountain Lakes

SUMMARY

① The setting of the base camp in the Peruvian Andes is described by Joe.

② We are introduced to Richard and how he came to be on the trip.

③ We are introduced to Simon, Joe's fellow climber, and they discuss the weather.

④ Simon and Joe attempt an acclimatisation climb on Rosario Norte but fail to reach the top.

⑤ Richard and Joe buy supplies from some locals.

⑥ Simon and Joe attempt to climb Cerro Yantauri but Joe falls and they stop.

⑦ They make a third attempt at another summit but again it is too difficult.

⑧ Joe, Richard and Simon journey to the foot of Siula Grande.

CHECKPOINT 1

How do the tales of Richard's travels help the reader get to know him?

WHY IS THIS CHAPTER IMPORTANT?

A It introduces the reader to why Joe loves climbing and to the knowledge it requires.

B It introduces the main characters in the story.

C It establishes the relationship between Joe and Simon.

D It hints at the dangers that the pair will face.

WHY AND HOW TO CLIMB

This opening chapter is important for helping the reader understand why somebody would choose to climb a mountain. The beauty of the mountain is established in the opening descriptions and Joe relishes the challenges and dangers. The chapter has many adjectives such as 'astonishing' and 'exhilarated'.

Joe describes each of the summit attempts in the chapter as a problem to be solved. He uses the character of Richard as the naive onlooker to explain the details of the climb. By using Richard in this way he allows us to understand without feeling patronised.

We learn of the potential hazards of cornices, the difficulty of walking on powdered snow and the issues of avalanches and the weather. Joe uses the test climbs to highlight these aspects so that the events of the main climb can be related with pace and tension, and without cumbersome explanation.

★ **GRADE BOOSTER**

It is important that you mention the impact of the writer's choices to get the top marks. How do you react to the events in this opening chapter? What are your reactions to the characters?

THE RELATIONSHIP BETWEEN JOE AND SIMON

In this chapter Joe is explicit about the close relationship he shares with Simon. He explains that he is 'glad' they had 'chosen to come ... as a two-man team'. Joe describes Simon as 'dependable' and 'sincere' and so makes it clear that they share a bond.

The friendship between Joe and Simon, and the trust they share, is an important theme in the book. Joe comments on the need for trust and a common approach to climbing when he explains the reason for not attempting the second test summit. He writes: 'Neither of us said anything about going straight down. It was an unspoken understanding between us that the summit would be left out this time.'

The fact that Joe emphasises the need for trust and complete understanding in the partnership means that we call into question the wisdom of the expedition. Early in this chapter Joe claims that there was 'something ... nagging at me, making me question him'. The reader is given the impression that conditions for the expedition are already in doubt as some aspect of this unspoken trust is missing.

KEY QUOTE

'There were few other people I could have coped with for so long.'

EXAMINER'S TIP: WRITING ABOUT DRAMATIC IRONY

The fact that Joe is the author makes it clear he survived the events described. Therefore, **dramatic irony** plays a part in the tension that the reader feels, especially when Joe keeps making reference to potential disasters during the test climbs. By focusing on one or two specific examples you can clearly show your examiner how this is meant to impact on the reader. For example, Joe states at one point: 'We had responsibilities to no one but ourselves now, and there would be no one to intrude or come to our rescue ...' This draws the reader's interest. How would they survive if there was no means of rescue? The use of the **ellipsis** is particularly effective in suggesting to us that we should reflect on this scary idea: if there is no means of rescue the only other outcome is likely to be death.

GLOSSARY

acclimatisation the need to get used to the thinner air at high altitude

cornice overhanging edge of snow that is extremely dangerous

Chapter 2: Tempting Fate

SUMMARY

❶ Joe describes the beginning of the climb.

❷ He describes climbing and how much he enjoys it.

❸ Joe and Simon see dangerous ice cornices overhanging the west face.

❹ There is a rock fall.

❺ Joe and Simon are forced to climb in the dark.

❻ Joe forgets to ask for an ice screw.

❼ They find a snow hole.

❽ When in the snow hole Joe recounts a story about falling whilst sleeping.

KEY QUOTE

'Simon was coming up, hitting hard, ice splintering down below him, hitting hard and strong, walking up on points of steel, head down, hitting, hopping ...'

WHY IS THIS CHAPTER IMPORTANT?

A It captures some of the rhythm of climbing.

B It introduces the theme of the thrill of adventure and danger.

C It uses motivational language.

THE RHYTHM OF CLIMBING

Joe cleverly uses language to recreate the rhythm of climbing in this chapter. This is really clear when the climbing is easy at the beginning of the chapter. Joe uses **repetition** of 'hitting' to match Simon's actions. The list of **verbs** such as 'hitting, hopping ... breathing' that Joe uses when describing this part of the climb gives a sense of fluent, assured movements. As this is an account of a real experience that happened in the past, Joe purposefully describes these actions using the present participle. Selecting to recount events in the present tense makes the actions feel immediate and therefore powerful.

The rhythm of the writing changes when the climbing becomes more difficult and dangerous. Joe uses simple sentences, such as 'I set off hurriedly', and then short phrases such as '80° maybe' to make his actions seem abrupt, rushed and uncertain.

KEY QUOTE

'I set off hurriedly ... I could see it was steep, 80° maybe, and hammered in a screw when I reached its base.'

DANGER AND ADVENTURE

An important **theme** in the book is the exploration of why people would choose to put themselves in danger. Even when the climb is going well Joe emphasises the discomfort and potential hazards of climbing. The chapter begins: 'It was cold.' The short, abrupt sentence emphasises the discomfort of this fact. However, Simon 'grinned' at Joe's pain from hot aches, and when they make lucky choices that spare them from getting hurt the language Joe uses seems excited: 'Thank God we hadn't climbed any nearer to the buttress!' The discomfort and fears seem a part of the challenge.

Joe seems to suggest that it is the emotion of being on a mountain and the sense of danger this creates that he enjoys. He describes 'a rush of exultation at being here' and when he feels a dragging sensation pulling him over the edge of the ice field he notes that he 'enjoyed the feeling'. There is a sense that the danger makes him feel alive.

GRADE BOOSTER

It is important to make links with other parts of the book. Is the sense of danger as appealing at the end of the book as it is in this chapter?

EXAMINER'S TIP: WRITING ABOUT MOTIVATIONAL LANGUAGE

The chapter is laced with short phrases that are meant to simulate Joe's attitude to the climb. By commenting on the use of the exclamation marks and the repetition you can comment effectively on **character**. For instance, Joe writes, 'Right then, this was it!' at the start of the main climb. Then, later when he had successfully climbed the first 150 feet and was feeling exhilarated, 'This was it!' By using exclamations he is trying to capture some of the challenge he feels when beginning such an adventure. The repetition of 'This was it!' suggests that this is truly what it means to be alive, and he is thrilled by the adventure.

GLOSSARY

hot aches
severe pain in the hands and feet caused by extreme cold

Chapter 3: Storm at the Summit

SUMMARY

① Joe and Simon meet a barrier of seracs.

② Simon falls a short way and Joe injures his mouth.

③ Joe admits to being afraid when climbing the gully becomes difficult.

④ They bivi over night when it is clear they won't make the summit.

⑤ Joe and Simon struggle up the flutings.

⑥ They reach the summit.

⑦ At the start of the descent there is a snow storm and Simon falls.

WHY IS THIS CHAPTER IMPORTANT?

A It reveals Joe's and Simon's characters in moments of difficulty.

B It explores the ideas of dreams and ambitions.

C The use of technical terms emphasises the writer's expertise and knowledge.

JOE AND SIMON REVEALED

This chapter is important in revealing the fellow climbers' characters and their relationship. Joe is presented in the opening chapter as thoughtful, keeping a journal of events and considering the negative impact of the weather. Yet in this chapter he allows fear to creep into his voice and he makes a careless mistake with the ice. Equally, although Simon is portrayed as someone who is easygoing and always smiling, in this chapter he is abrupt and pessimistic. Simon's only response to Joe's two attempted apologies after showering them both with ice is, 'I noticed.' Equally, Joe has to persuade Simon that there are possible routes when Simon sees the climb as 'desperate'.

The importance of the trust between the two climbers was introduced in the opening chapter but it is only when in the midst of troublesome circumstances that this is illustrated clearly. When Simon is testing routes up the gully Joe watches him 'carefully' and then later is 'tensed' for when he falls. There are many occasions in this chapter when Joe explains the importance of the rope between the two climbers, presenting it as a symbol of trust in the book.

DREAMS AND AMBITIONS

This chapter is important for its description of reaching the summit. It is the pinnacle of the exercise – as both men achieve the ambition of being the first to reach the summit of Siula Grande via the west face. Yet Joe himself describes the moment as an 'anticlimax'. The language that he uses matches this sense of anticlimax. He describes taking the 'customary summit photos', and then asks a series of questions, such as 'What now?' and 'Did I really want to come back for more?' This is not the elated language that you would expect of someone who has achieved an ambition.

EXAMINER'S TIP

To improve your marks consider alternative ways of looking at characters or discuss inconsistencies in the way they are presented.

Joe seems to be exploring the underlying reasons why people take on such challenges. He questions whether he does it for the sense of achievement or whether he is attempting to boost his own ego. The ultimate point he seems to be making is that once you achieve something difficult you must continue to strive for more dangerous things if you want to maintain a sense of purpose.

EXAMINER'S TIP: WRITING ABOUT THE TECHNICAL TERMS

Joe uses a lot of technical climbing terms in this chapter so it is necesssary to explore them. It is easy to ignore terms you do not understand but your examiner will expect you to consider their impact on the chapter. Unlike in the opening chapter Joe offers very little explanation of the language he uses and it is important to consider the impact of this on the reader. An example is, 'The whole slope was corrugated by powder flutings which had gradually built up as fresh snow had sloughed down the face.' The chapter has many terms related to the mountain or to climbing. Joe mentions 'seracs', 'flutings', 'cornices' and 'bivi', 'harness', 'ice screw'. This language helps to persuade us of his expertise and skill, whilst helping to draw us into the experience of climbing.

KEY QUOTE

'If you succeed with one dream ... it's not long before you're conjuring up another, slightly harder, a bit more ambitious – a bit more dangerous.'

CHECKPOINT 2

What would be the effect on Joe's story if he had used a vocabulary that all his readers could understand?

GLOSSARY

seracs
  clumps or pinnacles of ice that form in ridges on a glacier
bivi
  a temporary camp in an unsheltered area
flutings
  channels in mountains caused by erosion which form a ripple effect to look like corrugated iron
slough
  shed, as snakes slough their skin

Chapter 4: On the Edge

SUMMARY

1. Joe and Simon continue to walk along the damaged ridge.

2. Simon keeps descending, not noticing easier ground.

3. Joe crashes into Simon and they share an angry exchange.

4. They climb in the dark before digging a snow hole.

5. Simpson recounts an anecdote about some Japanese climbers.

6. They wake the next morning with only enough stores for one more meal.

7. Joe falls again and fears toppling over a cliff edge onto the west face.

WHY IS THIS CHAPTER IMPORTANT?

A It shows the relationship between the climbers when under strain

B It includes an anecdote to illustrate the increasing dangers they face

C It uses language to help build the tension

UNDER STRAIN

A lot of clues are revealed in this chapter about why the climb is destined to go wrong. Unlike earlier chapters where Joe takes time to describe how they study the mountain and make strategic choices, here the pair seem to be making ill considered and flawed choices. Joe describes the continued descent in the dark and storm. Simon's strategy for climbing is described as 'basic' and 'flawed' as he jumps down without knowing what he will land on. Joe later describes his own attempts using **verbs** such as 'scrabbled' and 'clawed'.

As the climbing technique breaks down, the relationship shows signs of strain. Joe and Simon exchange angry words when Joe slips and again when Simon makes an impetuous choice to continue downwards into dangerous territory. Later, Joe notes that the 'close intimacy' in the snow hole 'seemed odd despite how together we had been on the mountain', suggesting a possible distance between them.

KEY QUOTE

'Then, just as suddenly, I stopped, with my whole body pressed into the snow, head buried in it, with my arms and legs spreadeagled in a desperate crabbed position. I dared not move.'

ANECDOTES

Anecdotes are used throughout the book to help explain important features of climbing and to explore the possible mindset of the characters in the book. The anecdotes relate to incidents that both climbers have witnessed and experienced and which might have an impact on their outlook on the climb. The anecdotes are dramatic, usually illustrating the dangers that Joe and Simon are facing, and therefore heighten the tension.

In this chapter we learn of two Japanese climbers who fell to their deaths. One climber had fallen backwards off the face and the second had been pulled off by the rope. The belay piton had not held in the rocks. Joe recounts the anecdote in his book to give us the sense that he and Simon could have met a similar fate that day because of the dangerous choices they were making.

Joe provides this anecdote to help us understand the strength that Simon, who witnessed these events, possesses. Hearing this anecdote through Joe and not Simon means we are distanced from the full impact of such an incident. We want to know what Simon was thinking having nearly suffered a similar fate. If he had been narrating at this point he would have been expected to give us these details. The distance of the narrative perspective is important in keeping us interested as we can only guess at the fear this would cause or why he would continue to climb after such a trauma.

EXAMINER'S TIP: WRITING ABOUT THE INCREASING TENSION

This chapter is important in building the tension. The reader is anticipating a catastrophic disaster at any point and it is important for Joe to maintain the pace of the writing. When writing about this the examiner will expect you to understand how Joe does this, exploring a particular example in detail. Joe uses a mixture of powerful verbs such as 'pressed', listed phrases and short, abrupt sentences, such as 'I dared not move', to increase the pace of his writing.

GLOSSARY

impetuous
quick and not thought through
belay piton
a piece of metal that the climber jams between rocks and secures himself to using a rope

Chapter 5: Disaster

SUMMARY

❶ Joe walks across the cornice.

❷ He describes the ice cliff and the decision whether to descend it or go a long way around with limited supplies.

❸ Joe climbs down the ice cliff and falls.

❹ He suffers a shocking injury, breaking his leg, and discusses Simon's possible reactions to it.

❺ Simon himself describes his reaction to the accident and how he begins to go through the motions of checking Joe though he believes Joe will die.

❻ Simon then notes that he cannot leave Joe while he is still fighting to survive.

❼ Joe describes how he tries to carry on climbing.

❽ Simon begins lowering Joe down the mountain.

WHY IS THIS CHAPTER IMPORTANT?

A It examines further the themes of hope and fear.

B It describes the relationship between the two climbers in a dangerous position.

C It splits into two different narrative perspectives for the first time.

HOPE, FEAR AND DEATH

This chapter is interesting because of the changing reactions of Joe to his situation. There are times when the logic of the situation he is in overwhelms him and he claims to feel no 'fright' at the idea of dying. However, Joe's natural reaction is to fight. Simon describes how he looked back to see Joe contouring the cliff, how he was 'completely enclosed in his own private struggle'. It is at this point that Simon realises that he must help Joe, if Joe is choosing to help himself.

The fearlessness that Joe feels is closely linked to a lack of hope. When death is the only real option, Joe makes choices that are bold. However, Simon spots the col, seeing this as an end to some of their difficulties. With this chance of survival 'a surge of hope run[s] through [Joe] like a cold wind'. Joe suddenly sees that he could survive and wants to hang onto life.

CHANGING RELATIONSHIPS

The shift in narrative perspective allows us a unique insight into the changing relationship between the two climbers. When Joe initially falls and sees Simon approach he notices a look of pity in Simon's face. We later hear how Simon thought that Joe was a dead man. More powerfully, we hear from Simon how he left Joe and *forgot about him'*. It is as if to survive the shock Simon needs to distance himself from his friend. In contrast, Joe recognises that Simon would easily survive if he carries on alone and is too scared to ask for his help. His survival is now reliant on Simon's choices.

Once back into the pattern of descending the mountain some of the old relationship that was so important at the beginning of the book returns. Joe describes how *Simon nodded at me and grinned.'*

EXAMINER'S TIP: WRITING ABOUT NARRATIVE PERSPECTIVE

The examiner will be interested to see if you can explore the impact of the use of multiple narrative perspectives in this chapter. The most obvious reason for the different accounts is so that we hear Simon's side of the story. However, it is important to consider other less obvious effects of this choice. It could, for instance, symbolise a break in the partnership because their stories are no longer the same. It suggests that Simon will soon separate from Joe. Also, it puts us in a powerful position of knowing more than both narrators. Joe wonders what Simon's reaction will be. Simon has already described his seemingly harsh reaction and the reader feels some pity as we realise that he has emotionally distanced himself from his friend. The different narrative perspectives double the emotional intensity of the accident as we empathise with both men independently.

GLOSSARY

col
a pass between two mountains or a gap in a ridge – an area lower than the peaks that surround it

traverse
move sideways across a section of terrain instead of directly up or down

Chapter 6: The Final Choice

SUMMARY

❶ Joe fears that Simon is lowering him down the face too quickly.

❷ He describes the pain in his leg, the effort of digging the belay seats, and the effects of the cold.

❸ Simon shows great tenderness towards Joe.

❹ Joe falls over the edge and believes he will die from the cold.

❺ Simon now recounts lowering Joe down the face.

❻ Simon describes how he makes the choice to cut the rope holding Joe.

❼ Simon considers his reaction to his decision.

KEY QUOTE

'As he spoke he reached out and caught hold of my waist, tugging me gently towards him. He was careful, almost tender in the way he spun me round ...'

WHY IS THIS CHAPTER IMPORTANT?

A It explores Joe's state of mind.

B It gives Simon's justification for his actions.

C It contains allusions to religion.

JOE'S STATE OF MIND

Much of Joe's account in this chapter focuses on the pain and suffering that he endures as he is lowered down the face. Joe uses emotive language, such as 'hammering torture', and long lists of verbs, such as 'It snagged, and snagged again, twisted, kinked, and caused every sort of agony'; this captures the pain he experiences as he is lowered down the mountain.

However, much of what Joe has to endure is due to the cold. He describes having to push through the 'apathy' caused by the weather. When dangling over the edge, after falling, it is the cold that concerns him. He personifies the effects of the temperature, making it seem like an invading alien: 'I thought of it as something living; something which lived through crawling into my body.' Joe's thoughts as he dangles over the edge are fragmented. He uses incomplete sentences and ellipses to mimic his fractured thought processes. He writes: 'Won't be long now. I'll not last till morning ... won't see the sun either.'

SIMON'S JUSTIFICATION

The most powerful part of Simon's account in this chapter is his choice to cut the rope. In his mind he is sending Joe to certain death but he is decisive in his actions.

Simon's reaction to his decision is confused. At first he notes, *'There was no guilt, not even sorrow.'* However, when he is in his snow hole for the night he claims that it was *'necessary to prosecute myself, and to prove that I had been wrong'*.

Ultimately Simon concludes that he was right to cut the rope because otherwise he would have died. However, he is clearly confused and unhappy. The repetition of *'thinking'* shows that he is tormenting himself even though he believes he *'did right'*.

KEY QUOTE

'Had I killed him? – I didn't answer the thought, though some urging in the back of my mind told me that I had.'

EXAMINER'S TIP: WRITING ABOUT THE ALLUSIONS TO RELIGION 🔓

It is important to take notice of patterns of language and consider what this is meant to suggest to us. Simon makes some references to a higher presence when he gets ready to complete the climb the next morning. He claims that he *'dressed like a priest before mass'* and that he *'felt watched. Something in the crescent of the summits and ridges looked down on me and waited.'* The allusions to religion at the end of this chapter might suggest that he should be judged by a higher being than the reader. They might also suggest that he feels a greater sense of guilt than he is willing to admit to himself in his account of cutting the rope.

Chapter 7: Shadows in the Ice

SUMMARY

① Joe hangs from the rope waiting to fall.

② After the rope has been cut he falls fast, expecting to die.

③ He realises when he is in so much pain that he is still alive.

④ He cannot move because he has landed on an ice bridge.

⑤ Joe fixes an ice screw to the wall.

⑥ He reacts manically and rationally, in turn.

⑦ Joe comes to realise that the rope was cut.

⑧ He decides that he must abseil off the bridge or die.

WHY IS THIS CHAPTER IMPORTANT?

A It explores thought processes in a time of crisis.

B It contains a powerful description of the crevasse.

C It has a cliffhanger at the end.

THOUGHT PROCESSES

The opening of the chapter is characterised by the randomness of Joe's thought processes as he considers his situation. Joe powerfully captures the trivial thoughts that appear in someone's mind when they are in shock. When looking down into the crevasse he explains that his thoughts became slow and lazy. He looks into the crevasse beneath him and he describes the questions that run through his mind as 'idle'. The importance of this word is emphasised by its repetition and is matched by the series of simple sentences that slows the pace of the writing.

Before falling there is a dreamy quality to Joe's thoughts, as he focuses on the stars. He claims they were 'gemstones' and that they were 'winking ... on and off, on and off'. This slow and deliberate writing forms an effective contrast to the violence of the fall when he writes, 'A whoomphing impact on my back broke the dream'. The alliteration of the 'b' ensures a harsh change in tone.

> **CHECKPOINT 4**
>
> Joe dwells on the 'irony' of surviving a fall of 100 feet but with the knowledge that his climbing companion believes him dead. Why is this ironic?

THE CREVASSE

Joe's description of the crevasse emphasises the 'darkness'. He constantly repeats this word and calls it a 'black hole'. He makes the point that the darkness is 'impenetrable' and 'oppressive'.

At times it is almost as if there is something out there that could harm Joe. When he secures himself to the wall he claims that he is safe from the 'black spaces'. His laughter in the darkness is described as 'inhuman'. The hellish quality of the crevasse is emphasised when Joe describes it as having 'the feel of tombs' and as a 'space for the lifeless, coldly impersonal. No one had ever been here.' It is perhaps significant that he was attracted to this expedition because he would be one of the first people to achieve the climb, but this is now acting to isolate him.

Chapter 8: Silent Witness

Summary

1. Simon now describes his descent.

2. He finds the place where Joe fell over the edge.

3. He describes the ice cliff and abseiling down it.

4. He sees the crevasse that Joe has fallen into.

5. He explores the act of cutting the rope and the point of climbing the mountain.

6. Simon makes it to the glacier and then across to the moraines.

7. He decides he must tell the truth about what has happened.

Why is this chapter important?

A It allows Simon to explore the act of cutting the rope.

B It gives Simon's account, which seems to mirror Joe's experiences.

C It focuses on the point of taking on challenges.

Cutting the rope

One of the most important elements of this chapter is Simon's guilt at having survived and the problems he now faces having cut the rope. Throughout the book the rope has been presented as a **symbol** of relationship and trust between the two men and in some ways by cutting the rope Simon has damaged this for the whole climbing community. Although Simon would have died had he not cut the rope, by choosing to be proactive he may be accused of killing Joe. This is clear when Simon writes, *'I might as well have put a gun to his head and shot him.'* As Simon points out, he was in a situation where he could never win.

Simon's battle with his conscience at the end of the chapter is powerfully written. It contains questions such as, *'Why tell them that you cut the rope?'*; exclamations such as, *'I shouldn't have to face it!'*; and short sentences such as, *'I didn't kill.'* These combine to illustrate the confused thought processes that Simon is suffering.

KEY QUOTE

'No one cuts the rope! It could never have been that bad!'

MIRRORING

Chapters 7 and 8 seem to work together in the book. Chapter 7 is Joe's account after the fall and Chapter 8 is Simon's account. Such a distinct separation of the story is significant here as their journeys have taken such different paths.

However, many ideas that Joe uses in Chapter 7 are mirrored in Chapter 8. Simon begins his account with *'the sense of menace threatened to overwhelm me'*, which reminds the reader of Joe's description in the crevasse that seemed to suggest an evil presence. Equally, Simon claims that he was *'oppressed by the unnatural calm'*, as Joe had been by the silence in the crevasse. Yet more notable is the mirroring of emotional reaction to the accident, as if they are still bound by a common attitude. Both men are tormented, but also have their rational moments; and both men focus on the futility (total lack of purpose) of taking on such a challenge against a lifeless object, yet battle on to survive.

EXAMINER'S TIP: WRITING ABOUT A THEME

The idea of why someone would take on such a challenge is an important **theme** in the book. Joe touches on dreams and ambitions when he reaches the summit and again when in the crevasse, feeling the emptiness of a place where no one has been. Writing about a theme is about making connections across the book and addressing the overall message that we as readers are being asked to consider.

In this chapter Simon notes, *'This place was ageless and lifeless'*, and then exclaims, *'What a silly thing to pit oneself against!'* Like Joe earlier in the book, Simon questions the wisdom of taking on a challenge that requires you to beat something so inhospitable to life. The excitement and expertise required pales into insignificance when compared with the loss Simon feels. However, when connecting this theme across the book it is clear that the potential for death is the element that heightens the sense of challenge. In earlier climbs, Simon had witnessed the death of two Japanese climbers and Joe had fallen whilst sleeping. This makes us consider whether the dangers make living more exhilarating.

GRADE BOOSTER

Think carefully about what the similarities between Simon's and Joe's accounts might mean. Think what it might mean about human beings in general as well as Joe and Simon specifically.

GLOSSARY

moraines accumulations of boulders, stones or other debris carried and deposited by a glacier

Chapter 9: In the Far Distance

SUMMARY

❶ Joe lowers himself further into the crevasse.

❷ He reaches a thin floor of snow that should allow him to cross the crevasse and find his way out.

❸ He fights off the effects of pain to find a pattern of climbing.

❹ He makes his way out of the crevasse and back onto the side of the mountain.

❺ He realises that he still has 6 miles to go and will likely die on the way.

❻ Joe describes how he has two minds, and he chooses to listen to the commanding voice that tells him what to do.

❼ He sees the cut rope and realises Simon must think he is dead.

WHY IS THIS CHAPTER IMPORTANT?

A It explores the ideas of courage and fear.

B It captures some of the beauty and evil of the mountain.

C It contains images of good and evil.

COURAGE

The opening of this chapter is powerful in its exploration of bravery. For the reader it is clear that it takes great courage to lower yourself down into a hole of darkness. The determination to make such a choice – 'It was this, or nothing ...' – and commit to this course of action is an obvious act of bravery.

Yet, throughout the opening of this chapter, Joe repeatedly questions his own **character**. He notes that he does not have the 'courage for suicide' and then that he is not brave enough to look down into the hole. He is convinced of the idea that it is the desperation of not wanting a long drawn-out death that forces him into action.

The confusion of this battle between fear and courage is illustrated when Joe stops on the rope and cannot lower himself any longer. Before he could not look, and now he cannot help but look and perhaps it is the torment of being afraid that changes his perception of what is courageous.

KEY QUOTE

'I had to see what was beneath me because, for all my convictions, I didn't have the courage to do it blind.'

CONTRASTS

The chapter is characterised by contrasts. First, there is the beauty of the mountains and the horror of the situation that Joe finds himself in. This contrast is illustrated in the description of the crevasse with its 'vaulted ceiling' but also its 'shadows' and 'darkness'. It is further illustrated when Joe escapes the crevasse and notes the 'delicately fluted ridges' and the 'azure emptiness'. When he realises he has 6 miles to go before safety he notes that there is a 'tangible hostility' and 'This was not the playground we had walked into so long ago', suggesting that this is indeed a place of extremes.

These extremes are matched by Joe's emotional reactions to the situation. He notes himself that 'there were two minds within me arguing the toss'. This chapter is characterised by his deep despair and then by his determination and elation, meaning that much of the writing is **emotive**, using words such as 'terror' and 'mesmerised'.

EXAMINER'S TIP: WRITING ABOUT PATTERNS

Commenting on the writing of others is often about spotting patterns and showing curiosity at the reason for this. Talented writers rarely let such patterns emerge in their work by accident so it is the job of the reader to consider why they are there. Throughout this chapter, as in previous chapters, there is repetition of the word 'menace' and Joe claims the place is 'malevolent' or evil. However, this then contrasts with the description of the chamber which he suggests is like a church with its 'sacredness'. Joe seems to suggest with this pattern of images that there is a larger force at work and his confusion comes from wondering if it is good or evil. However, he concludes that there are 'no dark forces' acting against him, and it is his feeling of powerlessness that has made him want to believe he is being controlled by something bigger than him.

KEY QUOTE

'its magnificent vaulted crystal ceiling, its gleaming walls encrusted with a myriad fallen stones, shadows facing into darkness beyond the great gateway formed by the ice bridge'

CHECKPOINT 5

Joe uses the word 'playground' when describing his previous attitude to the mountain. What is the significance of this word choice?

GLOSSARY

azure
sky blue

Chapter 10: Mind Games

SUMMARY

❶ Joe slides down the slope to the glacier.

❷ He finds Simon's tracks and follows them across the glacier.

❸ He describes being pushed on by the voice to dig a snow hole.

❹ Joe is afraid of falling asleep.

❺ Simon takes up his story; he has returned to camp and is recuperating.

❻ He considers whether he murdered Joe.

❼ He burns Joe's clothes.

❽ Simon and Richard talk of the future.

WHY IS THIS CHAPTER IMPORTANT?

A It emphasises Joe's need to return to camp before Simon leaves.

B It contains references to Joe's life that allow us to care about his survival.

C It uses different voices to plot the narrative.

NARRATIVE HOOK

This chapter returns to a split narrative perspective. The first half recounts Joe's struggles to get off the mountain. The second half focuses on Simon's recuperation at base camp. This is known as a narrative hook. Joe, in his account, makes continual reference to his slow progress and the passing of time. In the chapter we are aware of another night passing.

Back at base camp Simon reports that he is *'bored with this place'* and we are made aware that he is likely to leave soon. The knowledge of both Joe's struggle and the way in which Simon and Richard deal with his possessions as though he no longer exists draws us into the book with a sense of powerlessness. We are forced into a situation of trying to work out how long Joe has been on the mountain and then how long Simon will stay.

JOE'S LIFE

The use of details from Joe's life back in England is a clever way of allowing us to get to know the man rather than the climber. This makes his struggle on the mountain much more human, as we empathise with him on our own level rather than that of an expert.

The strange mental state that Joe finds himself in, as he turns the ice cliff into a series of images, reveals that he is a cultured and intelligent man. He makes reference to religions and art that show he is educated and therefore not someone who would take on this challenge without consideration of the consequences.

However, it is references to his mother that are most powerful. He notes that 'I hoped that Ma was praying for me as she always did', which caused him to cry. The representation of Joe as someone's son makes it more emotional for us as we see the potential loss for his whole family.

KEY QUOTE

'They reminded me of pictures I had seen of the carvings inside a Hindu temple ... like the paintings by Titian of grossly fat nudes ...'

EXAMINER'S TIP: WRITING ABOUT EXTRACTS

In an exam, you might be encouraged to focus on extracts from the book. Joe's crawl across the glacier, with the contradictory voices in his mind and references to his life, would be a powerful extract to focus on. However, your examiner will be interested in your ability to connect this part of the story to the rest of the book. Joe has a difficult job making the laborious journey back to camp interesting for us. Therefore, he uses details of his life to sustain our interest. Also, the different voices that we hear are more extreme versions of his determination and exhilaration for life and the fear that grips him throughout the rest of the book.

Chapter 11: A Land Without Pity

SUMMARY

① Joe recounts a Shakespearean soliloquy he remembers in a nightmare.

② He worries about the lack of food and water.

③ He crawls on towards the moraines and gets lost amongst the boulders.

④ He begins to suffer from snow blindness.

⑤ He splints his leg and hops through the moraines.

⑥ He descends the cliff and is off the mountain.

⑦ Joe attempts to carry on to 'Bomb Alley' but has to give up and sleep.

WHY IS THIS CHAPTER IMPORTANT?

A Its Shakespearean soliloquy is important in revealing attitudes to death.

B It contains inhospitable descriptions of the landscape.

C It has an abrupt opening.

DEATH

Although Simpson recounts the soliloquy from Shakespeare because it appears in his nightmare, it is important to consider what it reveals about Joe's attitudes to death and what he may be trying to tell us. It is possible that Joe uses this allusion as a literary device to explore the theme of death.

The soliloquy comes from *Measure for Measure*. Claudio is condemned to death for making a woman pregnant out of wedlock. In some respects it could be said that Joe faces death because he sought pleasure doing something he knew to be dangerous. Claudio is commenting on how he fears death, not knowing what it will bring and how he views age with its 'ache' and 'imprisonment' as paradise in comparison. Joe may be suggesting that he too longs for the chance of old age in the face of his own death.

The fact that Joe claims to feel 'silly' after recounting the dream seems to suggest some folly in this thought of his death, that he is fearing death in the same way he fears the darkness – because it represents the unknown. Equally, he may merely feel foolish for reciting the soliloquy out loud.

CHECKPOINT 6

What is the effect of calling the area at the base of the mountain 'Bomb Alley'?

EXAMINER'S TIP

You do not have to think what the right response to the text is. A top-grade student is someone who can make judgements about the text, but always considers other possibilities and interpretations.

THE LANDSCAPE

The main focus of the chapter is the unforgiving nature of the landscape, as its title suggests. The terrain is difficult and each turn seems to offer no 'pity' to a painfully injured Joe, who struggles to get to base camp. Yet, there seems to be a lot of good fortune in Joe's ability to descend through the obstacles: for instance, he is lucky that there is a floor of snow covering the crevasse that allows him to escape.

Joe's description of the landscape emphasises its haphazard and extreme nature. He describes the section of the glacier as 'a broken mess of fissures and covered hollows' and how the moraines 'tumbled away from me in a wide torrent of boulders'. There is a sense in the use of 'broken' and 'tumbled' that Joe's perception has changed with the injury the mountain has caused him. His experiences have impacted on his view of the landscape and it now all looks beyond his control.
The idea that Joe feels at war with the landscape is further emphasised when he reaches the bottom of the cliffs. He claims that the cliffs are 'the doors to the mountains' and 'I had won a battle of some sort.' He feels as though getting off the mountain has put some of the 'menace' behind him.

KEY QUOTE

'Which way, which way? Over there ... and there I would crawl only to find myself dead-ended by another menacing fissure.'

EXAMINER'S TIP: EVALUATING LANGUAGE

Many of the chapters in the book open with a dramatic sentence to draw us into the events. The short, abrupt sentence at the beginning of this chapter is particularly effective. The examiner will expect you to comment on the impact of such opening lines as 'I awoke screaming.' You should consider your emotional reactions as you ask a series of questions about what could have happened to Joe now. It is also important to evaluate the negative impact of overusing such emotive phrases. It is possible that we could become desensitised to Joe's suffering if we are continually asked to empathise with such powerful emotions.

GLOSSARY

glacier
    a mass of ice slowly flowing over land
fissure
    a crack in the ice or rock

Chapter 12: Time Running Out

SUMMARY

❶ Simon recounts how Richard wants to leave base camp.

❷ Simon is reluctant to leave but agrees to do so the next day.

❸ They search for the money hidden by Simon and Joe before their ascent.

❹ Simon notes how sad the local girls are at Joe's supposed death, but want payment.

❺ Joe now recounts how he is exhausted and his motivational voice has become defeatist.

❻ Joe realises that Simon will leave soon and keeps going despite continually falling over.

❼ He finds water and manages to keep going when he senses he is close to camp.

❽ He calls out for Simon.

WHY IS THIS CHAPTER IMPORTANT?

A Narrative perspective is used to create dramatic irony.

B Richard is used as a plot device.

C It contains sentences which become shorter in order to build tension.

DRAMATIC IRONY

Multiple narrative perspectives are used effectively in this chapter to put us in a more knowledgeable position than the characters. At the most basic level we are aware of Joe's survival and proximity to the camp and of Simon's plan to leave soon. This creates a level of tension as we wonder if Joe will arrive back in time, even though we know that Joe must have survived.

Dramatic irony is used more specifically at the end of Simon's account. He describes how *'At about seven o'clock an eerie sound wailed out from the cloud-filled valley'*, and he and Richard dismiss the sound as a dog. Towards the end of Joe's account we hear how he called out for Simon – the knowledge that the sound Simon heard was Joe helps to build both our hope and frustration.

A more disturbing effect of this dramatic irony occurs when Simon searches for Joe's money to help pay for his trip back to Lima. We feel that Simon's actions are wrong – that he is stealing from Joe – even though we accept that Simon is convinced of Joe's death. Also, each time Simon makes reference to Joe's death we are put in a position of knowing that he is wrong in his assumptions.

KEY QUOTE

'Nine o'clock, eleven o'clock, the night stretched on, and the five hours' crawling from the moraine dam meant nothing.'

RICHARD

Richard's presence in the book is useful to Joe here, as it was in the opening chapter. At the beginning of the book Richard's lack of knowledge allows Joe to explain the background to the climbing trip to us. At the end of the book Richard is a useful plot device for pressing Simon to leave camp.

If Simon alone had been keen to leave he would appear an unforgivably cold character, as if running away from what he had done. Richard's insistence that they leave and Simon's reluctance to listen to him mean we still feel sympathy for Simon.

EXAMINER'S TIP: WRITING ABOUT BUILDING TENSION

The point of this chapter is to build the events in the novel to a climax. You will need to be able to talk about the way that Joe uses language to help this happen. Joe's account in this chapter recounts actions. Unlike previous chapters he does not focus on wider issues, as his whole focus is on moving towards the camp site. The sentences used tend to be short or contain a number of commas to help build the pace of the actions. The final paragraph mimics Joe's confusion. Joe uses a series of confused questions, and an incomplete final sentence acts to build suspense as to whether Joe will survive.

CHECKPOINT 7

On p. 212, in the section called 'Ten years on ...' Joe quotes a passage written by Simon. What does this passage tell us about the theme of trust and the importance of the symbolism of the rope?

GRADE BOOSTER

Even though the Foreword, Postscript, Ten Years On and Epilogue are not in the main part of the book they do offer important insights into the events. Read these sections carefully and note down anything that helps you to understand the ideas in the book better.

Chapter 13: Tears in the Night

SUMMARY

❶ Simon finds Joe close to camp and near to death.

❷ Joe thanks Simon and tells him he did the right thing.

❸ They share a moment of close friendship.

❹ Simon inspects Joe's leg.

❺ Simon and Joe have a conversation about Simon's decision to cut the rope.

❻ Simon, Joe and Richard leave the camp and go down the mountain.

❼ They hire a truck and take Joe and another man to a hospital in Lima.

❽ Joe is taken for an operation.

WHY IS THIS CHAPTER IMPORTANT?

A It contains a message from Joe about his opinion of Simon's actions.

B It shows that the strain placed on Joe's and Simon's relationship is not permanent.

C It contains a direct comparison between Joe and another injured man.

A MESSAGE TO THE READER

Joe has been clear that one of the reasons for writing the book is to give an account of the events so that Simon is cleared of any sense of guilt or wrongdoing. Throughout the book Simon has his chance to debate the moral decision he made to save himself by cutting the rope. Therefore, in many respects the audience for this final chapter is the climbing community who would have found the cutting of the rope such a terrible act.

Joe's first words to Simon when he meets him outside the camp include the word 'Thanks' and assertion that he 'did right'. In order to emphasise the point Joe says 'Thank you' one more time before explaining to Simon that he had saved his life. By repeating the message Joe makes it clear to us that he is grateful and not angry with Simon.

KEY QUOTE

Joe: 'How much he had been through I could only guess at.'

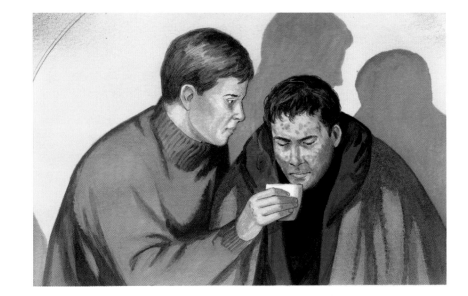

More powerful than the gratitude that Joe shows to Simon is the sympathy he has for him and the suffering he has endured. If Joe, who has had to climb down a mountain with a shattered leg, feels sympathy for Simon, then we have no choice but to feel empathy and not condemnation for Simon too.

THE RELATIONSHIP BETWEEN JOE AND SIMON

An important thread through the book has been the relationship between Joe and Simon. In the opening chapter Joe emphasises that they share a close bond that makes climbing together possible. Even when the narrative is separated there is a commonality of response that makes the two seem close.

In this final chapter Simon becomes 'stern and efficient' in caring for Joe and makes all the arrangements to get him to hospital. The conversations they share at the end of the book resemble the exchanges at the beginning of the book when they are organising the expedition, as if this is now another problem they must overcome.

However, more than anything in this final chapter, Joe focuses on the closeness of the friendship again. He points out that they now share 'a deep abiding friendship' and that 'every gesture, a touch on the arm, a look, an intimacy we would never have dared show before and never would again'. The experience seems to have strengthened their friendship rather than damaged the trust they share.

CHECKPOINT 8

In the Foreword, Chris Bonnington, a famous British climber, mentions other climbing disasters. How do these help us understand Joe Simpson's experiences in *Touching the Void*?

EXAMINER'S TIP: WRITING ABOUT SEEMINGLY UNIMPORTANT DETAILS

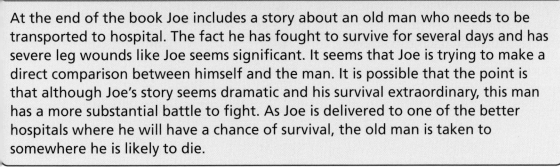

At the end of the book Joe includes a story about an old man who needs to be transported to hospital. The fact he has fought to survive for several days and has severe leg wounds like Joe seems significant. It seems that Joe is trying to make a direct comparison between himself and the man. It is possible that the point is that although Joe's story seems dramatic and his survival extraordinary, this man has a more substantial battle to fight. As Joe is delivered to one of the better hospitals where he will have a chance of survival, the old man is taken to somewhere he is likely to die.

Progress and revision check

REVISION ACTIVITY

① What are Joe and Simon attempting to climb? (Write your answers below)

....

② Why does Joe fall?

....

③ What does Simon choose to do that will upset many climbers?

....

④ How does Joe escape the crevasse?

....

⑤ What does Joe say to Simon in the tent at the end of the book?

....

REVISION ACTIVITY

On a piece of paper write down answers to these questions:

● What is the impact of knowing that Joe Simpson survives the events of the book?

Start: *As a reader we have more knowledge than usual so ...*

● How are multiple narrative perspectives used in the book?

Start: *Giving Simon a chance to tell his story means ...*

GRADE BOOSTER ★

Answer this longer, practice question about the action of the book:

Q: How does Joe Simpson ensure that the story is exciting for the reader? Think about ...

● The use of climbing terminology

● How Simpson begins and ends chapters

● How he uses different narrative perspectives

For a C grade: Convey your ideas clearly and appropriately (you could use words such as 'exciting' from the question and the bullet points to guide your answer) and refer to details from the text (use specific examples).

For an A grade: Make sure you comment on the varied ways Simpson makes the story exciting, and if possible come up with your own original or alternative ideas.

PART THREE: CHARACTERS

Joe Simpson

WHO IS JOE SIMPSON?

Joe Simpson is the author of the book and one of two climbers attempting to climb the west face of Siula Grande.

WHAT DOES JOE DO IN THE BOOK?

- Joe begins the ascent of Siula Grande with Simon (p. 15).
- Joe reaches the summit of Siula Grande via its west face (p. 44).
- Joe falls down an ice cliff and shatters his leg (p. 66).
- Joe is lowered down the mountain by Simon but falls into a crevasse when Simon cuts the rope (pp. 76–109).
- Joe escapes the crevasse (p. 141).
- Joe makes extraordinary efforts to crawl off the mountain (pp. 145–95).
- Joe makes it safely back to camp (p. 195).

HOW IS JOE DESCRIBED AND WHAT DOES IT MEAN?

Quotation	Means?
'I resolved to try some that very night.' (p. 4)	This is a response to Simon's hallucinations due to sleeping pills. For many the idea of hallucinating would be scary as they would feel out of control. For Joe it is the chance to find out what it is like.
'The sudden fright still had me breathing hard and it annoyed me to see Simon climb easily over the difficulties and know that I had lost control and let fear get the better of me.' (p. 38)	Despite the fact that he claims to have a strong bond with Simon and trust him, he still cannot allow himself to show fear to his companion. This might be a manly bravado where fear is seen as a weakness or it might be a sign in Joe's character that he cannot accept weakness in the face of anything.
'I looked back and was amazed to see that Joe had started traversing away from the cliff. He was trying to help himself by contouring round the small rise in front of him.' (p. 72)	Simon's comments about Joe reveal that he is extraordinary. Simon fully expected Joe to stay at the bottom of the cliff and accept his fate. He is inspired by Joe's fight and decides he should continue trying to help him survive the accident. Joe is presented here as an inspirational character who will not let obstacles get in his way.
'... like the paintings by Titian of grossly fat nudes that had mesmerised me at fourteen ...' (p. 149)	This proves that Joe is a fairly cultured and educated man because the reference to the painter is obscure for most people. However, the idea of a 14-year-old mesmerised by naked women is humorous and makes Joe appear human and likeable.

KEY CONNECTIONS

The book *Touching the Void* was made into a film starring Brendan Mackay and directed by Kevin Macdonald. Joe was asked to act some of the scenes on the mountain himself, including the scene where he crawls back to base camp.

 DID YOU KNOW

179 people have died in their quest to climb Mount Everest. There have been 1,924 successful ascents.

JOE SIMPSON continued

CHECKPOINT 9

In what ways could Joe be considered an unreliable narrator?

EXAMINER'S TIP: WRITING ABOUT JOE SIMPSON

Joe is the narrator of the story for most of the book. It is important to realise that there are a number of inconsistencies in Joe's character. At the beginning of the book he comes across as thoughtful but he later admits to making rash choices that cause the accident. He is in an immense amount of pain and at times delusional during the events he recounts. You should question Joe's account, considering how he may have reinterpreted the events to some degree. It is also important to point out the changes in Joe's emotions and mental state but more importantly his determination and strength to survive.

Simon Yates

WHO IS SIMON YATES?

Simon Yates is one of two climbers attempting to climb the west face of Siula Grande and takes some responsibility for narrating the events.

WHAT DOES SIMON DO IN THE BOOK?

- Simon begins to climb Siula Grande with Joe (p. 15).

- Simon reaches the summit of Siula Grande via its west face with Joe (p. 44).

- Simon slips off the edge of the ridge (p. 47).

- After helping Joe on the descent, Simon cuts the rope and allows Joe to fall (p. 101).

- Simon descends the mountain alone (p. 118).

- Simon meets Richard and tells him the truth (pp. 127–9).

- Simon finds Joe outside the tents at base camp and arranges for him to get to a hospital (p. 203–7).

KEY CONNECTIONS

Simon Yates has also written two books about climbing: *Against the Wall* and *The Flame of Adventure*.

How is Simon described and what does it mean?

Quotation	Means?
'I envied Simon his carefree take-it-as-it-comes attitude.' (p. 6)	Simon begins the book as someone positive and up for a challenge. He shows little concern for the weather patterns and is easily able to dismiss Joe's concerns.
'He was an easy friend: dependable, sincere, ready to see life as a joke ... that touch of madness which makes just a few people special.' (p. 6)	Joe is clear on what it takes to be able to climb with somebody. He defines Simon as someone who has all the qualities of a good climbing partner. You sense this description is the definition of somebody who would take on the challenge of an unclimbed mountain.
'He had an odd air of detachment.' (p. 69)	The warmth and friendship that Simon has shown in the book before this disappears when Joe hurts himself. This could be interpreted as coldness and a lack of humanity. However, in reality Simon was in shock and reacted in a way which allowed him to survive the situation. It is common for people to die from such injuries, Simon knew this and needed a way to protect himself.
'He had suddenly become stern and efficient.' (p. 198)	In some ways this shows that the transformation of Simon is complete. The easygoing character has gone and now he is someone who acts. The 'stern' reaction could be just an initial reaction to the shock and trauma. However, we are presented with a fundamental change in Simon's character by the end of the book.

EXAMINER'S TIP: WRITING ABOUT SIMON YATES

Simon's character is shaped by the events more than Joe's. He changes dramatically over the course of the book. It is important to focus on the contrasts in his character. At the beginning of the book he is optimistic and brave. He ignores Joe's caution about the weather. However, when on the mountain it is up to Joe to persuade Simon that there is a route, even though Simon more often than not takes the lead. At the end of the book Simon is shown as angry and confused, but then efficient in his help for Joe.

DID YOU KNOW

Climbing quickly in the mountains can cause pulmonary oedema. This is a build-up of fluid in the lungs caused by the change in pressure at altitude.

EXAMINER'S TIP

When writing about characters, remember they are created by the author, even if they are based on people who actually exist. Avoid referring to them as real people and instead consider the choices the author has made to help you understand their characteristics.

Richard Hawkings

WHO IS RICHARD HAWKINGS?

Richard Hawkings meets Simon and Joe in Lima and stays at the base camp throughout the main expedition.

EXAMINER'S TIP

It is easy to ignore a minor character such as Richard because he is not involved in the main action of the book. However, he plays an important role in the novel and your examiner will expect to hear about him in any general question on characters.

WHAT DOES RICHARD DO IN THE BOOK?

- Richards walks up to base camp and has altitude sickness (p. 3).
- Richard stays at base camp whilst Joe and Simon do test climbs (p. 6).
- Richard walks with Joe and Simon until the going gets too tough (p. 15).
- Richard looks after Simon on his return (p. 153).
- Richard presses Simon to leave for Lima (p. 172).
- Richard holds Joe's leg as Simon inspects the damage (p. 199).

HOW IS RICHARD DESCRIBED AND WHAT DOES IT MEAN?

Quotation	Means?
'He had lived off grubs and berries with pygmies while dug-out canoeing through the rainforests of Zaire, and had watched a shoplifter being kicked to death in a Nairobi market.' (p. 3)	Richard has the same sense of adventure as Joe and Simon. He clearly wants to experience the world and things that ordinary people would deem to be madness. This means that as well as the wonders of life, as represented by the canoeing, he has also experienced the other extreme of dangers and death. We realise this is not the first time he has experienced disaster on his journeys.
'I knew something terrible had happened. I'm just glad you managed to get down.' (p. 129)	This is Richard's reaction to Simon's honest retelling of the events. He appears not to be judgemental. For us, this acts as a model of how people should think about the events – Thank goodness somebody survived!
'Then he sat near me and talked of the long wait he had endured ... until he could bear the uncertainty no longer and had set out to find us.' (p. 129)	In some respects this reveals Richard to be a good and caring man. He could not walk away and leave them. The use of words such as 'endured' shows that for these men inaction is worse than reckless action. The likelihood is that if Richard had set off to find them in the mountains he would have been killed himself, as he was untrained and had no idea of the terrain.

EXAMINER'S TIP: WRITING ABOUT RICHARD HAWKINGS

Richard is a minor character in the book but plays an important part in helping us understand the events. He also represents the outside audience that Simon will have to face when he returns from the expedition. It is easier for us to empathise with Richard's reactions when one of the climbers does not return than it is to consider the reactions of people we have not met in the book. In effect, he acts as a plot device. A further example is in Chapter 12, when he causes us to realise that Simon will have to leave the camp.

GRADE BOOSTER

Try to increase your understanding of alternative perspectives on the events in the book by summarising the events from Richard's perspective.

The local villagers

WHO ARE THE LOCAL VILLAGERS?

These are a group of people who Simon, Joe and Richard call on for supplies and for help.

WHAT DO THEY DO IN THE BOOK?

- They give Richard a place to stay when he gets lost on the way to camp (p. 4).

  They sell homemade cheese (p. 12).

- The girls smile sadly at Simon, showing sympathy for his loss (p. 176).

  The girls expect to take some of Joe's possessions as they are no longer needed (p. 177).

  Spinoza haggles over the price of the mules that will get Joe off the mountain (p. 203).

THE LOCAL VILLAGERS continued

? DID YOU KNOW

Lima contains one-third of the population of Peru. One of the official languages of Peru is Spanish because it was colonised by Spain. Lima was founded by Spaniard Francisco Pizarro.

HOW ARE THEY DESCRIBED AND WHAT DOES IT MEAN?

Quotation	Means?
'Three-year-old Alecia guarded the entrance to the cattle enclosure, preventing the cows and calves from escaping ...' (p. 12)	A small child of 3 years would not be expected to do something so dangerous in our culture. However, Joe points out that these children are capable of looking after themselves and the harsh environment means they must grow up more quickly than western children.
'They angered me. What right did they have to feel sad?' (p. 177)	The local girls' reaction is used here to illustrate Simon's mental state. He has previously appeared quite pragmatic about the death of Joe and shown little emotion other than guilt. This reveals he is in shock and suffering a great deal at the loss of his friend.
'When Norma reached over and began sorting through the cooking utensils I exploded.' (p. 177)	This shows the cultural differences between Simon and the local girls. They see the sharing of Joe's things as pragmatic: Joe will no longer need the cooking utensils. For us, this is a shocking reaction to Joe's death, as we sentimentalise objects owned by the dead. Ironically, Simon and Richard have shown a similar attitude to Joe's possessions when using his radio and looking for his money, but for Simon this is different. The lack of personal connection to Joe makes the girls' attitude to his things offensive.
'There was some delay because Spinoza was being bloody-minded about payment for the mules.' (p. 203)	This seems unacceptable to us because Joe is clearly close to death and the local man is haggling for more money. However, Spinoza sees that the men in front of him need the mules he owns because one of them is badly injured. They are therefore likely to pay more because of the emergency and because there are no other mules available. Although we may consider this heartless, as we believe he should feel some humanity and want to help save Joe, in reality Spinoza has to fight for his own survival in a difficult landscape where such sentimentality has no place.

KEY CONNECTIONS

The film *K2* was released in 1991 and, although fictional, has a similar plot and themes to *Touching the Void*. Two men climb the second highest mountain when one falls and breaks his leg. The other lowers his friend to safety a few feet at a time.

EXAMINER'S TIP: WRITING ABOUT THE LOCAL VILLAGERS

The role of the local villagers is small in the context of the whole book. The most interesting role they play is in their reaction to the problems that the men face on the mountain. When Richard is lost he has to 'negotiate' for food and shelter. When Joe needs to get down the mountain when close to death, Simon must still strike a deal with the locals. As with the environment, there is little sense of compassion in these people – their job is survival and the outsiders bring items they need.

Progress and revision check

REVISION ACTIVITY

❶ Where did Joe and Simon meet Richard? (Write your answers below)

....

❷ What is Simon's reaction when Joe makes mistakes on the climb?

....

❸ How does Simon react to Joe's injury?

....

❹ What things creep into Joe's mind as he tries to get back to base camp?

....

❺ How do Joe and Simon react in the tent after Joe has returned safely?

....

REVISION ACTIVITY

On a piece of paper write down answers to these questions:

● What part does Richard play in the events of the novel?

Start: *Richard is important because he helps the reader to ...*

● How do the characters of Joe and Simon contribute to the events of the novel?

Start: *Joe and Simon can be said to be the cause of the events because ...*

GRADE BOOSTER ★

Answer this longer, practice question about the characters of the book:

Q: Compare Joe's and Simon's reactions to difficulties and explore what this reveals about their characters. Think about ...

● Both men's reactions to initial problems and difficulties

● Both men's reactions to the disaster that nearly ends their lives

● The anecdotes that Joe tells about previous disasters

For a C grade: Convey your ideas clearly and appropriately (you can use words such as 'difficulties' from the question to guide your answer) and refer to details from the text (use specific examples such as the moment where Joe hits out with his axe and covers both himself and Simon with sharp shards of ice).

For an A grade: Make sure you comment on the way that Joe's and Simon's reactions are revealed, such as their use of language in their different narratives of events. Try to come up with your own original ideas, such as considering why Joe wrote the book and how this reveals something about his reaction to difficulty.

Key contexts

THE AUTHOR: JOE SIMPSON

Joe Simpson is a climber, motivational speaker and author who was born in Kuala Lumpar in 1960 and lived in Gibraltar for part of his childhood. He now lives in Sheffield. Reading the book *The White Spider* by Heinrich Harrer, about an ascent of the Eiger, gave Simpson the inspiration to become a climber himself. As a young climber he would often attempt routes up mountains that were beyond his experience.

Touching the Void recounts real-life events that Simpson endured and which made his name both in the climbing world and as a writer. Throughout his climbing career he has experienced many other incidents, some of which he recounts as anecdotes throughout *Touching the Void*. He has written further books about these other climbs including *Dark Shadows Falling*, *Storms of Silence*, *This Game of Ghosts* and *The Beckoning Silence*.

Simpson was told he would never climb again after the accident in Peru but he has continued to climb and act as a mountain guide since. He recently climbed a difficult route in the Himalayas solo in memory of two friends.

A CENTURY OF DISCOVERY

The twentieth century was characterised by human need to explore and discover unknown lands. Mount Everest was climbed for the first time by Edmund Hillary and Tenzing Norgay in 1953, and in 1969 a man landed on the moon for the first time.

In *Touching the Void*, Joe describes the attempt made by him and Simon Yates to be the first climbers to ascend the west face of Siula Grande. Joe notes that *'the daunting 4,500 foot West Face had so far defeated all attempts'* (p. 2). The point is to go into battle with something that seems insurmountable. The book discusses this spirit of ambition, illustrated powerfully when Simon notes: *'It was a pointless thing to have done – climb up it, across it, and down it. Stupid!'* (p. 118), and later *'What a silly thing to pit oneself against!'* (p. 122).

CUTTING THE ROPE

Simon Yates faced a lot of criticism after the expedition to Siula Grande. He was the victim of many verbal attacks and was even physically assaulted on his return. He will forever held the title of 'The man who cut the rope'. Many climbers felt he had broken one of the most important rules of climbing by cutting the rope between him and Joe Simpson. Joe claims that part of the reason for writing the book was to exonerate Simon from the blame he received and to point out how Simon saved his life.

The rope between the two climbers in *Touching the Void* is presented throughout as a symbol of trust. Joe makes many references to the unspoken bond between the two men and how one will venture forward as the other stays back to protect him against a fall. There is much evidence in the book to suggest that this is a testimony in defence of Simon. He gets to tell his version of the events and at the end of the book Joe lies beside Simon and thanks him for saving his life.

CULTURAL DIFFERENCES

Siula Grande is in the Andes, in Peru, South America. As Joe points out in the diary extract at the beginning of the novel, this is a remote area where life is simple. The area was colonised by the Spanish because of rich mineral deposits in the mountains, but the region is largely agricultural and is now protected from further mining. The area is barely populated and is famous for trekking.

In the book the life of the locals seems starkly different from the western way of life. Young women are deposited by their father on the side of the mountain to tend his cows. They also care for their young children who take some responsibility for looking after the cattle, even at the age of 3. The locals' attitudes to the climbers and the accident contrast with the reactions of western readers to the tragedy. Their pragmatic approach is possibly characteristic of a people who are used to surviving harsh conditions.

KEY CONNECTIONS

In an article in *The Times* on 9 October 2003, Simon Yates explains what it is like to be labelled continually as 'The man who cut the rope'. He describes how he was verbally and physically attacked on his return to England.

CHECKPOINT 10

The villagers would have been used to outsiders walking and climbing in the area. How does this explain their reactions and attitudes in the book?

Key themes

FRIENDSHIP AND TRUST

At the beginning of the book, when taking part in test climbs, Joe points out that 'Neither of us said anything about going straight down. It was an unspoken understanding between us that the summit would be left out this time' (p. 10). There is a close bond between the men that means they can act without discussion.

The most potent **symbol** of this trust is the rope between them. When climbing near the summit of the mountain Simon falls off the ridge and it is only because Joe had been cautiously watching at the other end of the rope that he survives the fall. This is what makes the cutting of the rope such a symbolic act, as it appears to break the unspoken trust that climbers must share to climb successfully together.

It is the survival of this friendship that is one of the most inspirational aspects of the book. Joe is keen to point out that Simon saved his life and the act of writing the book was a defence of his friend. This is clear at the end of the book when Joe repeats his gratitude to Simon, claiming, 'You saved my life you know', and then, 'Thanks for getting me down' (p. 201).

GRADE BOOSTER

When considering the question 'What is the book about?', you need to avoid simply recounting the plot. Think about the ideas that Joe is exploring with his story about climbing Siula Grande.

EXAMINER'S TIP: WRITING ABOUT FRIENDSHIP

When writing about friendship it is important to separate the men's initial reactions to the disaster and the bond they share. It is easy to view Simon's reaction as cold and lacking in care as he points out how he forgets his friend. In reality he has to forget Joe sitting at the bottom of the cliff with a broken leg if he is to concentrate on the dangerous climb he has to complete to retrieve the rope. It is easy to select evidence from his account that could condemn Simon as a bad person. In some respects the reader must trust Joe at the end of the book when he describes an intimacy in their friendship that resulted from their joint survival of such a disaster.

REVISION ACTIVITY

Reread the following episodes. Consider what they tell you about friendship.

- An unspoken understanding that they would stop the test climb (p. 10)

- The trust needed to climb (p. 34)

- Simon finds Joe at the bottom of the ice cliff (p. 69)

- Joe thanking Simon (p. 201)

SPIRIT OF ADVENTURE

It is difficult for some people to understand what drives people to do extreme activities such as climbing to the top of mountains. In some respects Joe explores what motivates people such as him to go on adventures to places others haven't been before – wondering if it is pleasure or egotism that pushes him. Simon claims that it is *'pointless'* and *'stupid'* (p. 118) when he is descending alone after the accident.

The drive to try new things seems to be a significant part of this. At the opening of the book Joe describes how Simon experiences vivid hallucinations due to the sleeping tablets he is taking, to which Joe claims, *'I resolved to try some that very night'* (p. 4). He seems intent on experiencing life in a way that most of us would find frightening.

Indeed, the danger seems to be an important part of this spirit of adventure. When reaching the summit Joe describes the experience as an anticlimax. He states his concern: *'If you succeed with one dream, you come back to square one and it's not long before you're conjuring up another, slightly harder, a bit more ambitious – a bit more dangerous'* (p. 44). He concludes that ultimately the only end to this adventure will be his own death as he tries something beyond his ability.

> **KEY CONNECTIONS**
>
> Joe Simpson has written other climbing books including *The Beckoning Silence*. This book explores in more detail the effects on him of the deaths of friends and how they overshadow the rewards of climbing.

EXAMINER'S TIP: WRITING ABOUT THE SPIRIT OF ADVENTURE

The sense of adventure in the book is closely linked to the **characters** of Joe and Simon. The reader is asked to wonder why people would take up such a challenge and why they would continue to do this when they have experienced such loss. The changing emotions of the climbers should help you to explore this idea. Your examiner will expect you to notice the exhilarated responses to the challenge at the beginning of the book. You should also point out that Richard's reaction to their failures is explored by Joe, who is perhaps trying to illustrate that an outsider would not understand. The response to the climb becomes downbeat when they reach the summit and becomes more questioning when disaster hits. The change in the characters' reactions after the disaster means they even start to question what they are doing. The examiner would want you to consider if this event has changed the characters completely or whether the **anecdotes** included by Joe show us that they are likely to climb again.

REVISION ACTIVITY

Reread the following episodes. Consider what they tell you about the spirit of adventure.

- Enjoying the sense of danger (p. 19)
- The anecdote about falling when sleeping (p. 27)
- Reaching the summit (p. 44)
- Simon describing the challenge as a stupid thing to undertake (p. 118)

SURVIVAL

Both men have to do extraordinary things to survive the events of the book. The story is an inspirational tale of what it takes to overcome massive obstacles and challenges. The ordinary reader would feel throughout that they are likely to have given up and died at the first hint of pain and suffering.

For Simon Yates the act of survival is a matter of making a choice to cut the rope connecting him to his friend. Simon writes about this himself when he claims, *'I had done it, and done it well'* and *'That takes some doing! A lot of people would have died before getting it together to do that!'* (p. 103). Joe too would probably have died if Simon had procrastinated, and in some ways survival is a result of Simon's decisiveness.

For Joe Simpson survival is a process of overcoming physical and psychological barriers. Initially there is the pattern of movement that he develops to move from place to place despite the intense pain he is suffering. More importantly there is the fear of the unknown and the opposing urges in his mind that debate between giving up and driving on.

CHECKPOINT 11

Would you have cut the rope? Would you have told the truth about cutting the rope?

REVISION ACTIVITY

Reread the following episodes. Consider what they tell you about survival.

- Joe beginning to hop down the mountain (p. 73)

- Simon lowering Joe down the mountain (pp. 76–80)

- Cutting the rope (p. 101)

- Joe crawling down the glacier (p. 146)

NATURE

The contrasting beauty and cruelty of the mountain is an important **theme** of the book. On a superficial level there is an **irony** that the aspects of the mountain that drew Joe and Simon to the challenge of the climb become almost insurmountable on Joe's journey down. An example of this is the moraines at the foot of the mountain which are an intriguing puzzle to begin with and then become a dangerous maze later.

This contrast seems to take on a religious significance at times as the landscape is described as *'an evil force'* (p. 119) or is compared to a cathedral, with the crevasse in which Joe is trapped having *'a feeling of sacredness'* and a *'magnificent vaulted crystal ceiling'* (p. 137). Both Joe and Simon describe a sense of 'otherness' as though there is something spiritual about the mountain.

At other times the mountain is just seen as an inanimate object. In anger Simon describes their trek up the mountain as stupid because it is merely an aging piece of ice and rock. The chapter 'A Land Without Pity' best sums up the reality of the situation, as this is an extreme environment and the challenge comes from the difficulty in overcoming it.

REVISION ACTIVITY

Reread the following episodes. Consider what they tell you about nature.

- Simon feeling nothing for the beauty of the mountain (p. 118)
- The beauty of the crevasse (p. 134)
- The malevolent landscape and conditions (p. 152)
- The menacing fissures (p. 161)

> **EXAMINER'S TIP**
>
> When writing about themes and ideas in the book it is helpful to use connectives such as 'furthermore', 'therefore' and 'also' to make sure you are adding enough detail to your points.

Progress and revision check

REVISION ACTIVITY

1 Why does Joe believe he can climb with Simon? (Write your answers below)

....

2 What happens to Simon at the summit?

....

3 What does Joe notice when he wakes up in the natural snow hole?

....

4 Why can't Simon leave Joe straight after the accident when he has broken his leg?

....

5 How does Joe get through the boulders?

....

REVISION ACTIVITY

On a piece of paper write down answers to these questions:

● What does Simpson suggest is the point of climbing the mountain?

Start: *Simpson talks a lot about why he climbs the mountain and when he reaches the summit, he claims ...*

● What does Simpson suggest it takes to be courageous?

Start: *When on the ice bridge Simpson points out that ...*

GRADE BOOSTER ★

Answer this longer, practice question about one theme of the book:

Q: Explore what Simpson writes about facing challenges. Think about ...

● How the characters in the book solve problems

● Joe's reaction to the difficulties he faces

● Simon's reaction to the difficulties he faces

For a C grade: Convey your ideas clearly and appropriately (you can use words such as 'challenges' from the question to guide your answer) and refer to details from the text (use specific examples such as the way Joe tests a pattern that will allow him to climb out of the crevasse).

For an A grade: Make sure you comment on the way that Simpson reveals his opinion on what it takes to face challenges, for instance the fact that he doesn't give a definite answer but asks a lot of questions. You should try to come up with your own original and alternative ideas, such as considering how Simpson uses different voices to show the internal battle that Joe faces.

PART FIVE: LANGUAGE AND STRUCTURE

Language

Here are some useful terms to know when writing about *Touching the Void*, what they mean and how they appear in the book.

Literary term	Means?	Example
narrative hook	When the writer hints that something dramatic is going to happen.	At the beginning of the book Joe claims, 'We had responsibilities to no one but ourselves now, and there would be no one to intrude or come to our rescue ...' (p. 8). We sense that they may need rescuing at some point in the expedition.
dramatic irony	When the audience knows more about what is happening than some of the characters.	The different narrative perspectives, when Simon and Joe tell their stories separately, allow us to know more than both characters. When Joe looks at the end of the rope and wonders if Simon cut it we know that he did.
personification	When things or ideas are treated as if they are people, with human attributes and feelings.	Joe describes the cold as something living when he claims, 'I thought of it as something living; something which lived through crawling into my body' (p. 97).
imagery	Language which uses images to make actions, objects and characters more vivid; metaphors and similes are examples of imagery.	When hanging from the end of the rope Joe describes the stars, claiming, 'you'd think them gemstones hanging there, floating in the air above' (p. 107).

MOTIVATIONAL LANGUAGE

Joe's character is best captured at the beginning of the book. He uses many phrases to encourage himself to overcome the challenges he is about to face. This shows that he is a strong character who does not like to admit defeat. This is clear when he says, 'This was it!' (p. 18) and later 'Take a few breaths and get on with it!' (p. 24). The short phrases and exclamation marks illustrate his exuberance and energy.

Such language is mirrored in the dialogue between Joe and Simon. Their clipped phrases and exclamations illustrate the need for clear exchanges between people. This is illustrated when Simon takes control after the accident and claims, 'I'll go ahead and make a trench' and later 'Come on! I've got the rope' (p. 78).

★ **GRADE BOOSTER**

Being able to use the names of literary devices in your answers makes you sound more confident in your analysis. You should practise writing sentences that include terms such as climax and dramatic irony; make it seem as if they are a part of your everyday vocabulary.

REPRESENTING THE DIFFERENT VOICES

When attempting to escape the mountain Joe describes the 'voice' that helps him to know what to do. He uses language in such a way as to help us understand the difference between this commanding voice and the lethargic mental state that he finds himself in at times.

'The voice' that Joe hears uses short, clipped phrases, which rely heavily on **imperatives**, for example, *'Place-lift-brace-hop ... keep going'* (p. 167). In contrast, when he is overcome with pain and cold the sentences become long and like a list, for example, 'I had no sense of time passing, and with each fall I lay in a semi-stupor, accepting the pain and quite unaware of how long I had been there' (p. 168).

Simon's narrative also uses language differently. Throughout the book Simon has quite an abrupt style of speaking. When Joe makes a mistake that causes Simon to be showered in shards of ice, he replies to Joe's explanations with a sharp 'I noticed' (p. 38). This abrupt style is matched in his narrative, where he considers the rights and wrongs of his actions clearly and rationally.

LANGUAGE TO BUILD TENSION

Joe uses a number of devices to help build tension in the book. The first is the **narrative hook**. He alludes to disasters or potential difficulties that lead us to wonder if this is the way that events go wrong for the climbers. This is clear at the beginning when Joe has a niggling concern about the weather that he ignores.

Joe also builds tension with the use of short sentences or phrases and **repetition**. He makes some of the description of climbing sound breathless and difficult. This is clear when he is lowered by Simon after the fall. He writes, 'I *had* to stop. I realised that Simon would hear nothing, so I must stop myself' (p. 92).

Finally, once disaster has hit, Joe uses questions to raise doubt about what will happen to him. Although we are aware that he must have survived due to the completed book we are reading, the intensity of his doubt makes us tense and unsure of how he will survive. This is clear when he is hanging from the rope and asks, 'I wonder how deep I will go? To the bottom ... to the water at the bottom?' (p. 106).

EXAMINER'S TIP

When referring to language you must always quote the specific part of the text that you are talking about.

EXAMINER'S TIP

Your examiner is interested in your ability to read into the words selected by the writer and to try to understand how he or she must have been feeling. This is called empathising and is an important reason why we study literature.

EXAMINER'S TIP: WRITING ABOUT WORDS

Writing about language need not involve complex terminology such as **dramatic irony** or **imagery**. At times it is just as effective to focus on the words Joe employs. If you do this specify the sort of words you are going to focus on – whether it is his choice of adjectives that capture his reaction to the landscape or the quality of the **verbs** he uses to give some indication of his attitudes and emotions to his predicament. For instance, he 'lolls' at the end of the rope and 'fumbles' when things get tough but will 'hit' and 'kick' when he feels in control.

Capturing the beauty and cruelty

Joe uses language powerfully to capture the landscape. One of his strategies is to call upon our senses to let them experience the world he is in. For instance, when describing the collapse of the pillar that he slept on in a previous expedition he emphasises the magnitude of the noise: 'The thunderous sound of tons of granite plunging down the pillar echoed and then died to silence' (p. 28).

Joe also uses imagery to help us see the world as he does. On his downward trek he reaches the moraines and notes a 'dark river of rock flowing away from me' (p. 164). This partly captures Joe's desperation for water at this point but also gives us an image of a long line of rocks curving to and fro in front of him. The idea of the rocks 'flowing away' suggests that they go on for a long time and appear beyond his control.

Finally, both Joe and Simon make the landscape come alive at times. The **personification** of the mountain gives it a power over them and highlights their lack of control over this extreme environment. For instance, Joe has to persuade himself on his descent that 'dark forces' (p. 144) are not working against him.

DID YOU KNOW

The symptoms of hypothermia include a lack of coordination, confusion and sluggish thinking. Many of the contrasting thoughts that appear in Joe's mind could be a result of hypothermia.

GRADE BOOSTER

Select a random page and random line number. Find a quotation and think carefully about what you might write about it.

Examiner's tip: Writing about contrasts

When writing about contrasts it is important to find examples of both the extremes that you are discussing. You should then explore each of the quotations, considering what impact the language choice is meant to have. A good example of this is the contrasting emotions that Joe feels when he is in the crevasse. At some points he appears elated because of the cold: 'I giggled more, listened and giggled again' (p. 111). The repetition of 'giggled' makes this seem hysterical. In contrast, 'Part of me recognised this; a calm rational voice in my head told me it was the cold and the shock' (p. 111). The more controlled sentence construction means this mimics the 'calm' that he speaks of in the sentence.

Structure

THE PRACTICE CLIMBS

Although some readers will be experienced climbers, many will have no understanding of the extreme dangers or the landscape that Joe and Simon face. Joe uses these opening climbs to explain some of this to us and he can later assume that we understand the situations that arise.

THE OPENING AND CLOSING OF CHAPTERS

The opening and closing stages of chapters are used to capture our attention. Most chapters end with the closing of a day but occasionally Joe ends when he has made a bold choice, making us wait to know the consequence of this decision. Equally, the opening of a chapter is often very dramatic, for instance, 'I awoke screaming' (p. 156). We are immediately 'hooked' as we wonder what disaster has befallen Joe now. Even simple openings such as 'It was cold' (p. 17) serve to capture our attention as the blunt style feels conversational, as if we are hearing Joe speak.

CHANGING NARRATIVE PERSPECTIVES

The most powerful structural device employed by Joe is the changing narrative perspective. To hear Simon's version of cutting the rope and his descent is important for the intentions of the book – to persuade people that he made the right choice.

However, the changing perspectives also put us in a position of knowing more than the characters in the book. So when Joe wonders at Simon's choice, we are already aware of what Simon has been thinking. The perspectives also allow for dramatic pauses between action, for instance at one point Joe is lowering himself down into the crevasse with no knowledge of where he will land. At this point we must wait to know what happens whilst Simon recounts his descent.

THE USE OF TIME

Towards the end of the book Joe increases the tension by using time. Throughout his accounts Simon talks of waking up, and gives us a sense of another day passed. Joe does the same.

Joe's sense of time becomes confused. This is emphasised as Joe makes a reference to his watch and makes it clear that something could have taken him ten minutes or five hours. Richard's pressure on Simon is also a clever device for making us concerned about whether Joe's battle for survival will be futile.

EXAMINER'S TIP: WRITING ABOUT OVERALL STRUCTURE

It is important to link the overall structure to the themes that Joe is exploring. In some respects the book is split in two, with two climactic moments. The first part of the book focuses on the dangers from taking on challenges such as this, which climaxes with Joe's accident. The second part focuses on what it takes to survive, with the climax being Joe's eventual arrival at base camp.

CHECKPOINT 12

We know that Joe survives because he has written the book. However, Joe is asking us to feel frightened for him in case he does not make it to base camp in time. Why is this successful when we know he must have made it back?

EXAMINER'S TIP

When talking about the structure of the book it is easy to fall into telling the story. Keep description of the events to a minimum and instead focus on how the story is written and why it is written that way.

★ GRADE BOOSTER

What sort of diagram would best represent the story in the book? Draw the diagram, labelling it with the important parts of the story.

Progress and revision check

REVISION ACTIVITY

❶ What technical terms are used to describe the landscape in the opening chapter? (Write your answers below)

....

❷ How does Joe describe the sky just before Simon cuts the rope?

....

❸ What sort of punctuation does Joe use to show that he is in pain at the bottom of the ice cliff?

....

❹ When Simon begins his account after Joe has fallen down the ice cliff what do we know that he doesn't?

....

❺ What time does Joe think it is when he is approaching base camp?

....

REVISION ACTIVITY

On a piece of paper write down answers to these questions:

● What is the impact of the opening chapter?

Start: *Simpson uses the opening chapter to help the reader by ...*

● How does Simpson use the structure of the book to make the reader concerned for his survival?

Start: *There are two important moments when Simpson cleverly organises events to concern the reader: the first is ...*

GRADE BOOSTER ★

Answer this longer, practice question about the structure of the book:

Q: Explore the impact of the multiple narrative perspectives on the reader's reaction to the events. Think about ...

● The reader's attitude to Simon's choice
● How it adds to the drama of the events
● What it tells us about climbing and surviving accidents

For a C grade: Convey your ideas clearly and appropriately (you can use words such as 'perspectives' from the question to guide your answer) and refer to details from the text (use specific examples such as the way Simon uses his account to say he had done the right thing).

For an A grade: Make sure you comment on how the perspectives are used. For example, in the middle of the book Joe and Simon are given a chapter each to show that their journeys are now completely separate. You should try to come up with your own original ideas, such as considering the similarities in the narratives and what this shows about human beings in difficult situations.

Understanding the question

Questions in exams or controlled conditions often need **'decoding'**. Decoding the question helps to ensure that your answer is relevant and refers to what you have been asked.

 ### UNDERSTAND EXAM LANGUAGE

Get used to exam and essay style language by looking at specimen questions and the words they use. For example:

Exam speak	Means?	Example
'Explore ...'	*'Provide lots of detail on different ideas.'*	Joe provides different views on adventure. At times he notes the exhilaration that makes him feel alive. Yet, at the summit, he says the continual drive to take on challenges will eventually kill him.
'How ...?'	*'Look at the techniques used by the writer.'*	Explore how Joe communicates his ideas. For example, early in the book he asks, 'I wonder how much of this I really believed' (p. 5). By acting as an unreliable narrator he encourages us to question events.
'close reference to the text'	*'Look carefully at quotations or a small part of the novel.'*	When Joe falls after the rope is cut he describes the physical effects: 'I couldn't breathe. I retched. Nothing. Pressure pain in my chest' (p. 108). The short and incomplete sentences mimic the fractured thoughts and shock that Joe feels.

 ### 'BREAK DOWN' THE QUESTION

Pick out the **key words** or phrases. For example:

Question: Explore how Simpson captures the **need** for **adventure** in *Touching the Void*.

● You should 'explore how', e.g. discuss and provide your own ideas

● The focus should be on the need for adventure

What does this tell you?

● **Focus** on the techniques used to make us understand and empathise with the need for adventure, e.g. the use of imperatives, repetitive language, multiple narratives and anecdotes.

KNOW YOUR LITERARY LANGUAGE!

When studying texts you will come across words such as theme, symbol, imagery and metaphor. Some of these could come up in the question you are asked. make sure you know what they mean before you use them.

Planning your answer

It is vital that you **plan** your response to the controlled assessment task or possible exam question carefully, and that you then follow your plan, if you are to gain the higher grades.

 ## DO THE RESEARCH!

When revising for the exam, or planning your response to the controlled assessment task, collect **evidence** (for example, quotations) that will support what you have to say. For example, if preparing to answer a question on how Joe Simpson explores the theme of nature you might list ideas as follows:

Key point	Evidence/quotation	Page/chapter, etc.
Joe can experience the power of nature as something spiritual.	'I was mesmerised by this beam of sunlight burning through the vaulted ceiling from the real world outside.'	Chapter 9, p. 134

 ## PLAN FOR PARAGRAPHS

Use paragraphs to plan your answer. For example:

❶ The first paragraph should **introduce** the **argument** you wish to make.

❷ Then, jot down how the paragraphs that follow will **develop** this argument. Include **details**, **examples** and other possible **points of view**. Each paragraph is likely to deal with one point at a time.

❸ **Sum up** your argument in the last paragraph.

For example, for the following task:

Question: How does Joe Simpson present the character of Richard? Comment on the language devices and techniques used.

Simple plan:

● Paragraph 1: *Introduction*

● Paragraph 2: *First point*, e.g. An example of someone else who is adventurous

● Paragraph 3: *Second point*, e.g. Someone who needs an explanation of climbing terminology

● Paragraph 4: *Third point*, e.g. A presence at the end of the book who Simon must explain events to

● Paragraph 5: *Fourth point*, e.g. A plot device pushing Simon to leave

● Paragraph 6: *Conclusion*

How to use quotations

One of the secrets of success in writing essays is to use quotations **effectively**. There are five basic principles:

❶ Put quotation marks, e.g. ' ', around the quotation.

❷ Write the quotation exactly as it appears in the original.

❸ Do not use a quotation that repeats what you have just written.

❹ Use the quotation so that it fits into your sentence, or if it is longer, indent it as a separate paragraph.

❺ Only quote what is most useful.

TOP TIP USE QUOTATIONS TO DEVELOP YOUR ARGUMENT

Quotations should be used to develop the line of thought in your essays. Your comment should not duplicate what is in your quotation. For example:

GRADE D/E | GRADE C

(simply repeats the idea)	(makes a point and supports it with a relevant quotation)
When he abseils down Joe didn't want to return if it led to nothing. He says, 'if there was nothing there I didn't want to come back.'	Joe seems to suggest that he has given up when he abseils down and points out that 'If there was nothing there I didn't want to come back.'

However, the most sophisticated way of using the writer's words is to embed them into your sentence, and further develop the point:

GRADE A

(makes point, embeds quote and develops idea)
Joe takes a fatalistic view of what's ahead of him when he decides to abseil down from the ice bridge, facing the idea that if 'there was nothing there,' he 'didn't want to come back.' In this way, he demonstrates both courage and fear simultaneously.

When you use quotations in this way, you are demonstrating the ability to use text as evidence to support your ideas – not simply including words from the original to prove you have read it.

Sitting the examination

Examination papers are carefully designed to give you the opportunity to do your best. Follow these handy hints for exam success:

 ## BEFORE YOU START

- Make sure that you **know the texts** you are writing about so that you are properly prepared and equipped.

- You need to be **comfortable** and **free from distractions**. Inform the invigilator if anything is off-putting, e.g. a shaky desk.

- **Read** and follow the instructions, or rubric, on the front of the examination paper. You should know by now what you need to do but **check** to reassure yourself.

- Before beginning your answer have a **skim** through the **whole paper** to make sure you don't miss anything **important**.

- Observe the **time allocation** – and follow it carefully. If the paper recommends 45 minutes for a particular question on a text make sure this is how long you spend.

 ## WRITING YOUR RESPONSES

A typical 45 minutes examination essay is between 550 and 800 words long.

Ideally, spend a minimum of 5 minutes planning your answer before you begin.

Use the questions to structure your response. Here is an example:

Question: Do you see the ending of the book as negative or positive? What methods does the writer use to lead you to this view?

- The introduction to your answer could briefly describe **the ending** of the book;

- the second part could explain what could be seen as **positive**;

- the third part could be an exploration of the **negative** aspects;

- the conclusion would **sum up your own viewpoint**.

For each part allocate paragraphs to cover the points you wish to make (see **Planning your answer**).

Keep your writing clear and easy to read, using paragraphs and link words to show the structure of your answer.

Spend a couple of minutes afterwards quickly checking for obvious errors.

 **GRADE BOOSTER**

Where appropriate refer to the language technique used by the writer and the effect it creates. For example, if you say, 'this metaphor shows how ...', or 'the effect of this metaphor is to emphasise to the reader ...' this could get you higher marks.

'KEY WORDS' ARE THE KEY!

Keep on mentioning the **key words** from the question in your answer. This will keep you on track AND remind the examiner that you are answering the question set.

Sitting the controlled assessment

It may be the case that you are responding to *Touching the Void* in a controlled assessment situation. Follow these useful tips for success.

WHAT YOU ARE REQUIRED TO DO

- Make sure you are clear about:
- The **specific text** and **task** you are preparing (is it just *Touching the Void*, or more than one text?)
- How **long** you have during the assessment period (i.e. 3–4 hours?)
- How **much** you are expected or allowed to write (i.e. 2,000 words?)
- **What** you are **allowed to take** into the controlled assessment, and what you can use (or not, as the case may be!). You may be able to take in brief notes BUT NOT draft answers, so check with your teacher.

GRADE BOOSTER

Produce a list of at least three key moments, three key quotations and three opinions of your own on each character.

HOW YOU CAN PREPARE

Once you know your task, topic and text/s you can:

- Make **notes** and **prepare** the points, evidence, quotations, etc. you are likely to use.
- Practise or draft **model answers**.
- Use these **York Notes** to hone your **skills**, e.g. use of quotations, how to plan an answer and focus on what makes a top grade.

DURING THE CONTROLLED ASSESSMENT

Remember:

- **Stick** to the **topic** and task you have been given.
- The allocated **time** is for **writing**, so make the most of it. It is double the time you might have in an exam, so you will be writing almost **twice as much** (or more).
- If you are allowed **access** to a **dictionary** or **thesaurus** make use of them; if not, don't go near them!
- At the end of the CA follow your **teacher's instructions**. For example, make sure you have written your **name** clearly on all the pages you hand in.

Improve your grade

It is useful to know the type of responses examiners are looking for when they award different grades. The following broad guidance should help you to improve your grade when responding to the task you are set!

GRADE C

What you need to show	What this means
Sustained response to task and text	You write enough! You don't run out of ideas after two paragraphs.
Effective use of **details** to **support** your **explanations**	You generally support what you say with evidence, e.g. when exploring the idea of the voice you select quotations such as *'Get moving ... don't lie there ... stop dozing ... move!'* (p. 161)
Explanation of the writer's **use of language, structure, form**, etc., and the **effect on readers**	You write about the writer's use of these things. It's not enough simply to give a viewpoint. So, you might comment on the use of ellipses indicating pauses between comments to show that they happen all the time; the use of imperatives to stress commands; the use of an exclamation to show the determination in the voice.
Appropriate comment on **characters, plot, themes, ideas** and **settings**	What you say is relevant. If the task asks you to comment on how Joe reacts to difficult situations you focus on his character and how he survives. You might mention the split voice in his head; the references to his family; the patterns of movement; his reflections on cowardice.

GRADE A

What you need to show in addition to the above	What this means
Insightful, exploratory response to the text	You look beyond the obvious. You might question the philosophical views that Joe explores, such as when at the summit he comments on the motivation of those who explore dangerous places.
Close analysis and use of **detail**	If you are looking at the writer's use of language, you comment on each word in a sentence, drawing out its distinctive effect on the reader, e.g. 'We chattered out our alarm in quavery voices; quick staccato curses and repeated phrases tumbling out before we calmed' (p. 61). The verb phrase 'chattered out' suggests an expulsion of emotion and inarticulate conversation. Equally the use of the verb 'tumbling' shows how out of control they feel in the face of danger. Cleverly, Joe creates the sound pattern of their conversation.
Convincing and **imaginative interpretation**	Your viewpoint is likely to convince the examiner. You show you have *engaged* with the text, and come up with your own ideas. These may be based on what you have discussed in class or read about, but you have made your own decisions.

Annotated sample answers

This section provides you with extracts from two **model answers**, one at **C grade** and one at **A grade**, to give you an idea of what is required to achieve at different levels.

> **Question:** Read from page 107 ('I lolled on the rope ...') to page 108 ('I could see nothing.') Answer both parts of the question:
>
> **A** How does Simpson help the reader to feel the dramatic nature of the fall in this passage?
>
> **B** How does Simpson show his changing emotions during his fight for survival in the book as a whole?

CANDIDATE 1

Good use of words from the question to keep the answer on track

Good specific reference to the text

Simpson makes this passage dramatic in the way that it is all calm at first and then suddenly it is panicky. It is calm before because he is commenting on the stars and calls them 'Old friends come back.' He suddenly falls and Simpson makes this seem sudden by using the word 'Then' and the word 'pounced' which sounds like he is being attacked.

The fall is clearly dramatic because he seems to shout. He writes 'Ahhh ... NO!' He uses capital letters to show that he is shouting and the exclamation mark helps. He is frightened of falling into the crevasse and this shouting shows how scared he really is.

This point is a little obvious and there are more original ways he shows the drama

This could have been a direct quotation from the book

Using words like 'probably' shows a lack of confidence

It is also dramatic when he lands because his emotions keep changing, like he doesn't know how to react. He is crying and laughing at the same time, which is a weird way to react. This is probably because he is in shock because of what has just happened to him.

The changing emotion he shows here also happens through the rest of the book. It becomes a little stranger because he describes how there is a voice that is separate from him. He points out at one point that he is 'split in two' and that the other part of him is telling him what to do.

A good point but this needs to be explored more

Good use of quotation within a sentence

A good comment on character

Overall, Simpson is really determined. The best example of this is when he reaches the boulders and can't crawl anymore so he uses his mats to act as a splint to keep his leg supported and then hops through. So, even when he is really upset and suffering from pain and the cold he can make choices that will help him to survive.

> **Overall comment:** This is focused on answering the question, with some well chosen quotations. Some of these quotations are discussed well though there is clearly room for some more detail. The comment about Simpson's 'split' thoughts could have been developed more to explore how people have a natural instinct for survival.

GRADE C

CANDIDATE 2

This gives the sense of a whole answer to the questions – dealing with the ideas together

The focus is on the reader's reaction to the language chosen by Simpson

Good use of specific techniques employed by the writer

The comment is developed further

The comment is developed further

Continued reference to the text shows an excellent knowledge of the book

Clever use of quotation

An intelligent link to an important theme in the book that draws the point to a conclusion

This is an imaginative exploration of the novel that is strongly focused on the needs of the reader

The passage where Simpson falls after the rope is cut is characteristic of much of the book from this point on. The narrator provides a dramatic contrast between his feelings of calm and feelings of panic. Before the fall Simpson focuses on the environment around him: the description of the stars is a clever way of lulling the reader into the security of the rope, as the writer's words are almost poetic, describing them as 'gemstones' and romanticising their beauty. The use of 'Then' alters the tone immediately, dramatically illustrating to the reader that something has happened. The use of the verb 'pounced' cleverly reveals the violence of the action, as Simpson suggests he has been attacked. This is supported by the short, abrupt sentences that describe the physical assault he endures: 'I couldn't breathe. I retched. Nothing. Pressure pain in my chest.' The writing mirrors the disjointed sensations he must have felt as he fell into the crevasse.

This use of contrast is consistently used throughout the rest of the book, most notably to describe the emotions that Simpson is feeling. This is shown most powerfully when he notices that he still has a long way to go after escaping the crevasse. He first notes that 'I had never felt so entirely alone' and then soon after 'I felt thrilled as adrenalin boosted through me.' Simpson seems to be characterising what it means to survive a difficult situation such as this. He has a 'voice' that naturally drives him to act and chemicals coursing through him that propel him forward. The 'split' comes when his mind brings doubt and fear at the situation he is in. The battle to survive seems to be much more psychological than physical, as the narrator shows himself constantly swaying between such extremes.

The serious situation he finds himself in is also contrasted by the absurdity of the song that repeats in his head. He hears 'Brown girl in the ring ... Tra la la la la ...' The silly repetitive pattern seems odd when Joe faces death. This strangeness of thought patterns is also highlighted when Joe looks at a wall of ice and imagines paintings of nudes he enjoyed as a 14-year-old boy. The technique of using random thoughts effectively highlights his psychological state in this position but also adds a dark humour that keeps the reader from becoming drained by the struggle to survive.

Overall comment: This response explores the idea of contrasts in detail. Both parts of the question are addressed clearly but there is a sense that this is one whole response being discussed. References to the text are integrated into the discussion and technical terms such as 'verb' are used confidently.

GRADE A

Further questions

EXAM-STYLE QUESTIONS

❶ Explore the importance of the chapter headings in *Touching the Void*.

❷ How does Simpson maintain the interest of his readers when they know he survives?

❸ Compare the characters of Simon and Joe and their reactions to the events in *Touching the Void*.

❹ Explore how *Touching the Void* is evidence of the human spirit of adventure.

❺ Look closely at Chapter 1 of *Touching the Void*. How is language used to show the extreme conditions that the characters experience in the novel?

CONTROLLED ASSESSMENT-STYLE QUESTIONS

❶ Explore how the characters change in the book you have studied.

❷ Explore the role of fear in the book you have studied.

❸ Explore how structure plays a part in keeping the reader engaged in the book you have studied.

❹ Select a key extract from the book you have studied. Explore its importance to the book as a whole.

❺ Explore how the book you have studied represents the attitudes and ideas of the time it was written.

Literary terms

Literary term	Explanation
alliteration	the repetition of a consonant sound
allusion	an indirect reference to someone or something
anecdote	a short story used to illustrate an idea or point
character(s)	either a person in a play, novel, etc., or his or her personality
cliffhanger	a part of a book that is very exciting or frightening because the reader is left not knowing what will happen next
climax	a peak of action or excitement in a book
dramatic irony	when the reader knows more about what is happening than some of the characters
ellipsis	three dots (…) used to show that a word or words have been left out
emotive language	words and phrases that imply a lot of emotion
imagery	descriptive language which uses images to make actions, objects and characters more vivid in the reader's mind; metaphors and similes are examples of imagery
imperative	verb used at the beginning of a sentence to act as a command
irony	the difference between what is expected and what actually happens
narrative hook	a device used to arouse interest and intrigue in the reader
narrative perspective	the viewpoint of the person who is telling the story
personification	when an inanimate object or idea is given human qualities
plot device	a tool used by the author to make the story work
repetition	when an author repeats a word or phrase for a particular effect
soliloquy	when a character in a play speaks directly to the audience as if thinking aloud, revealing their inner thoughts, feelings and intentions
symbol	an object used to represent another thing or idea
theme	a central idea examined by an author
unreliable narrator	when the narrator might not be in a state to understand how events really occurred
verb	an action or doing word

Checkpoint answers

Checkpoint 1
The tales from Richard's travels make him seem adventurous and with a similar madness that Joe finds appealing in Simon. He has seen both sides of adventure – exciting times in a canoe and then the horror of watching his companion get shot dead.

Checkpoint 2
Although the reader would more easily understand the events, the use of simple terms would make Joe seem like an amateur. Also, the text would be too dense, as he would have to use many more words to capture what he was doing.

Checkpoint 3
Whether Simon is harsh or not is a matter of opinion. It appears heartless, as though he has decided to save himself and leave his friend. Realistically, however, Simon would not be able to continue the dangerous descent if he dwells on the probable death of his friend.

Checkpoint 4
Joe points out that surviving 100 feet relatively unscathed is fairly miraculous. However, he is likely to die anyway because Simon believes he is dead. This is ironic because if you survive such a massive fall you could expect to survive anything.

Checkpoint 5
The word playground suggests that Joe and Simon viewed the mountain as a place to have fun. It implies that their attitude was childish and naive.

Checkpoint 6
'Bomb Alley' is the name that Joe and Simon gave to the area at the base of the mountain on their way up. The suggestion is that the mountain is already attacking them and they are at war with nature. This is mirrored in Simon's comment on the futility of taking on a lifeless object such as a mountain.

Checkpoint 7
Simon points out that there are different opinions about whether he should have cut the rope. He explains that if he had waited much longer he would have endangered his own life. He points out that if he hadn't broken that symbol of trust both he and Joe would have been dead now.

Checkpoint 8
Bonnington tells these stories of survival and death to point out the danger that all climbers accept as part of their pastime. He reminds us that Joe's story is more compelling and drastic than the examples he gives because he survived to write it himself.

Checkpoint 9
Joe is unreliable in the sense that he suffers from hypothermia and is in severe pain for the latter part of the book – he reveals the incoherence of his thoughts in his writing. The story is told by Joe some time after his return so he has had a chance to shape the events to suit his desire to tell a certain story. Although he is honest about the mistakes he and Simon made on the climb we may wonder how much he wants to excuse himself for the events. He does give us permission to doubt his perspective when he claims at the beginning that he is unsure of the honesty of the details in his diary.

Checkpoint 10

The locals will see the climbers as an opportunity to make money. The area is known for trekkers so they know that people such as Simon, Joe and Richard need supplies and are likely to pay much more than they are worth to the villagers because they have little choice of where to get support.

Checkpoint 11

At the time the book was written cutting the rope was the most controversial element in it. Some of the climbing community were of the opinion that a climber should never cut the rope. Simon and Joe both claim in the book that it was the right thing to do because both would have died if Simon had not. In some respects we have to applaud Simon's decisiveness and his will to survive.

Checkpoint 12

Even though we know Joe gets back to base camp we do not know how. This is part of the tension that Joe creates, as we wonder how much more he must do to survive. Furthermore, we empathise with Joe's fear of the possibility that Simon has left. Knowing that it is a close call increases our sense of empathy for Joe as we realise his fears are well founded.